What Would You Have Said?

Rose Riso
73 Romora St,
Pittsburg, 94565
432-4362

What Would You Have Said?

Witnessing with Confidence and Sensitivity

Nellie Pickard

Foreword by Howard G. Hendricks

BAKER BOOK HOUSE
Grand Rapids, Michigan 49516

Copyright 1990 by
Baker Book House Company

ISBN: 0-8010-7113-5

Printed in the United States of America

To my grandchildren
(according to age):

Anne, Nathaniel, Esther, Ruth, Elizabeth, Reuben, Karen,
and **Jonathan.**

Your God-given abilities amaze and delight me.

My prayer for you
is that you will serve Jesus Christ
and use the gifts he has given you
to honor and glorify his name.

Contents

What Would You Have Said—

8

Foreword

Witnessing is a worrywart for many Christians. We revel in the revolutionary life-changing gospel of joy and hope. Somebody told us, so we know it is transferable; yet it sticks in our throats when the time comes to talk about it. It's a paradox; we want people to know our Savior, but we find ourselves mute, distracted, and blundering in the face of unbelief.

Jesus himself showed us how to use normal encounters when he met the Samaritan woman at the well and changed her life with a single conversation. He left us with a charge to follow his example and spread the Good News. We are, he said, his witnesses throughout the world.

To help us Nellie Pickard has ably come to our aid with *What Would You Have Said?* From Uncle Earl to her scientist-neighbor she takes us into her laboratory and lets us listen in on what to say. Nellie is a "natural," and she nudges her readers toward commonplace opportunities. Sharing our faith is far more than a duty; it's a high privilege, and this book shows us that it is entirely "do-able." It's a volume that does not belong on the shelf. It begs to be read, to be discussed, and to be passed along to another Christian. The world is hungry for the message.

Howard G. Hendricks
Dallas Theological Seminary

Preface

I am greatly humbled as I hear from people who have been helped by reading my first book, *What Do You Say When?* . . . You'll meet some of these people in this book. As I witness, sometimes I make wise decisions, sometimes not so wise. God in his mercy doesn't cast me aside as a useless tool but teaches me through experiences the better way. I'll tell you more about some of the lessons I learned along the way. Often I'm amazed at God's patience with me.

May this book challenge you to witness effectively and easily in your own way and in your own circumstances.

Acknowledgments

I am indeed grateful to God for accomplishing in me that which just a few years ago I would have deemed impossible. My thanks to my friend and former pastor, Joe Stowell, who helped me to see that if I did the possible, God would do the impossible.

I want to thank my beloved husband, Paul, my best friend and teammate in the Lord's work. Paul's patience in proofreading *everything* I write, taking care of the tax work, and being responsible for the sale of the books after I speak takes a load off my back. I appreciate his going with me when I speak and considering it fun. In using his spiritual gift of helps, he has been a good role model and an inspiration to me. Thank you, Paul, for being God's tool in this way.

Introduction

A woman recently asked, "How do you get started in witnessing? Do you just walk up to someone and start talking about the Lord?"

"No," I replied, "I have learned to be alert and sensitive to whatever the situation. I usually ease into a conversation. Then see what it leads to."

"How do you know it's the right time to speak?" she asked.

"The Spirit of God directs me. I don't know how to describe it, except it seems to be a gentle nudge. I don't believe in collar grabbing or hitting people over the head with the gospel. I believe that's of the flesh. I never argue with people, and if a person doesn't seem interested, I don't try to get my point across."

I learned the above principles the hard way. I wasn't always sensitive to people's needs. Many times I barged in where "angels feared to tread." That was early in my Christian life.

My Uncle Earl was not a Christian. As a zealous kid, I sang hymns right at him during family get-togethers. And then boldly announced, "Uncle Earl, you've got to accept Jesus Christ as your Savior. If you don't, you'll go to hell!"

Uncle Earl glared at me, his loving face now set like flint.

"Well, Nellie, I've chosen the way I want to live, and you've chosen yours. I have *not* chosen your way."

I'll never forget the finality in his voice. I knew I had

offended him. I dearly loved him, but I had not been tactful nor acted in love.

Even though I was in my early teens at the time, I've never forgotten the sting of that encounter.

For a while I lost my enthusiasm for witnessing.

As I grew in my Christian experience, I realized that witnessing was not an option; it was something God wanted me to do.

I asked the Holy Spirit to be my instructor. It's been the best course in evangelism I've ever had.

When Jesus met the woman at the well, they got into a conversation concerning water. It was very natural for Jesus to begin talking about the "living water." That was something he could give her. The Samaritan woman was puzzled and started to ask questions.

Jesus could turn any conversation around. He wanted those he talked with to be concerned about their relationship with the Father.

"How and who do you worship?" was always his probing question.

Jesus taught that worship must be in spirit and in truth. It must come from the heart—not the things we do and don't do.

I am aware of Christ's tenderness with the woman at the well. He reminded her of her many affairs with men but didn't lambaste her or denounce her severely for her lifestyle. He offered her "living water" that would satisfy and take away the guilt of the past. He didn't come into the world to condemn it but to save it (John 3:17).

I learned much from studying this passage, and asked God the Holy Spirit to make me more Christ-like in my approach to witnessing.

Jesus did not spare the Pharisees however. He called them hypocrites. They appeared to be righteous on the outside but on the inside were full of hypocrisy and wickedness. They faked their godliness (Matt. 23:27). He could say that because he knew their hearts.

When the Jehovah's Witnesses come to my door, I can refuse them welcome because I know their doctrine. It's against the truth of God's Word. They will not listen when I quote Scripture to them. They twist the truth and deny the deity of Christ. They are a false witness.

I learned a lot when I signed up to be used at a Billy Graham Crusade as a counselor. There I discovered that witnessing was on-the-job training.

Depending on the pure truth of God's Word, I was trained here to use the following plan. The staff reminded us not to take anything for granted.

"Just because people respond to the invitation," our instructor said, "doesn't mean they understand the step they are taking. Be sure you go through the Scripture we've given you, step-by-step."

I found memorizing verses most profitable.

Man is sinful—Romans 3:23

Sin has a penalty—Romans 6:23

Christ paid the penalty—Romans 5:8

Salvation, a free gift—Ephesians 2:8,9

Christ is our salvation—John 10:9

We must receive him—John 1:12

The old zeal for witnessing now has handles. I can grab ahold of God's message and share it without fear of offense.

One evening at the crusade I simply asked a woman, "Do you believe the Bible when it says, 'For all have sinned and fall short of the glory of God'?" (Rom. 3:23).

I'll never forget the look she gave me. Tearfully she said, "That's why I came forward. I need to be forgiven."

The rest was easy. I read the verses, and she responded.

God took all of these experiences and expanded them. He has been with me wherever I go.

Sometimes we just sow the seed as we have opportunity to witness. God wants us to be faithful in all of our acts for him, whether it be sowing, watering, or reaping. We must never forget: Only God can bring the increase.

1

What Would You Have Said—

When You Discovered Your New Wall Hanging Had Idols on It?

"Let me help you carry the groceries," my husband said as he greeted me at the door. "I'm starved. Hope you plan to have something good for dinner."

"Before I prepare something to eat, I have to tell you about the wall hanging I saw today. In fact, I brought it home—on approval, of course. It's in the trunk of the car, if you'd like to get it."

"Tell me about it while you fix dinner. I'll put the groceries away."

I was so excited I had a hard time concentrating on what I was doing. "Well, I saw this beautiful oriental rug at the import store on Woodward Ave. It will be just perfect for the living room."

We had been looking several months for the appropriate wall hanging for this particular room. I felt I had found it and hoped my husband would like it as well as I did.

I looked at him to see what his reaction would be. I couldn't tell, so I went on. "I talked to the manager, and he said I could take the rug home on approval. All I had to do was to sign a paper saying it was in my possession. They had other rugs too, but not nearly as nice as the one I brought home."

"Okay," he said, "but let's eat first. Then we'll take a look at it."

I was sure he would like it once he'd seen it. I ate my dinner hurriedly. I felt like a kid with a new toy.

"Why don't we go out for a hot-fudge sundae before we look at your prize?" Paul said with a twinkle in his eyes. He knew how much I liked hot-fudge sundaes but he also knew that was not important to me right then.

"Come on now, stop your teasing."

We hung the rug on the wall in a temporary fashion, and Paul seemed pleased. "It certainly goes well with the colors in the room. I like the oriental figures in it too."

"Can we buy it?" I asked.

"If you like it—go ahead and get it."

I could hardly wait until the next day. The carpet company was the first errand on my agenda.

The manager greeted me with a smile. "How did your husband like the wall hanging?" he asked.

"He liked it very much and said I could get it."

"By the way," the manager said, "I have papers that give the background of where the rug came from and the dynasty it represents. It tells quite a story."

"Now that will make it quite a conversation piece," I said. "I'm eager to get back home so my husband can hang it."

It had been a long time since I'd gotten such a lovely piece for our house. It would be the finishing touch for our new home. As my husband was preparing to hang the rug a bit more permanently, he said, "Read the papers that came with it. Let's see what kind of a story we will be able to tell our friends when they come to visit."

I eagerly started to read. "The figures on the rug represent five Chinese *idols* . . . my voice trailed off into nothingness. "*Idols!* Who wants idols on the walls?" I asked. Then as if in defense I said, "But those idols don't mean a thing to us. We don't worship them."

"But, Nellie, that wall hanging is making a statement in our home. Do we want it to be about idols? And if our friends ask us what the figures on the rug are, what would you say? Would you feel comfortable telling them they are idols?"

I knew he was right but I was angry at the salesman. *If he hadn't given me those papers everything would have been just fine,* I thought.

I knew what I had to do but I wasn't happy about it. I reluctantly brought it back. In its place I bought another rug, very nice, but it couldn't compare with the oriental one.

When I got home, I noticed Paul was doing some calligraphy. He looked as though he was ready to frame it. "What are you doing?" I asked.

"As I was thinking about the oriental rug," he said, "It occurred to me, we should have a statement of faith in our home—something that represents *our* faith. Since this is close to the Fourth of July and everyone is celebrating the Declaration of *Independence* why don't we celebrate our *dependence* on God? Look, what do you think of it?"

I read:

Declaration of Dependence

Having been adopted by the most high and holy GOD into his family, through his SON who gave his life to redeem us from destruction, we hereby declare our desire to submit to the loving authority of JESUS CHRIST in all matters of faith and practice.

Because of who he is,

Paul E. Pichard
Nellie Pichard

21

"I'd like us both to sign it," he said.

"I agree. That will be our statement of faith for our home." I knew it was the right thing to do.

Our Declaration of Dependence was hung in the foyer of our home, where it can be easily seen by anyone who enters.

I was pleased with the plaque, but every once in a while I'd get a hankering for that beautiful oriental rug. I was still miffed at the salesman for giving me the papers telling me about the idols!

About six months later we had two young men come to clean our carpets. One of the men kept looking at our "Declaration of Dependence." He seemed a little hesitant; then as he shifted from one foot to the other, he said, "I like that." He then looked at the floor and repeated, "Yeah, I like that."

"It's our declaration of dependence on God. Do you have faith in God? Do you know Jesus Christ as your Savior?"

"Yeah, it just happened last week," he said nervously.

"Tell me about it." I asked.

"Well, you see, it was like this. I was on drugs. I mean I was really gone on drugs. Life was worth nothing. My friend came to my rescue and told me how I could be forgiven of my sins. He introduced me to Jesus Christ. I asked him to come into my heart and forgive me. I believe in him now. That's why I like that [pointing to the plaque] 'cause that's what I want to do—depend on him."

I don't have a hankering for the wall hanging anymore. God showed me something better: doing that which honors him.

The interesting point is, I thought the oriental rug would be the conversation piece but it could never have stimulated the discussion that was started over the simple motto declaring our faith in God. Some have commented, "I would like something like that in my home."

Looking Back

Many times since then I have thought, *If I could see as God sees, I'd make better choices in life.* But then I realize that's not living by faith. We must choose the best way in life while we have the chance to do so. I didn't deserve it but God allowed me to see the result of the more excellent way.

I now realize that my problem wasn't so much the idols on the rug—as it was the rug itself. It had become an idol. I wanted something I shouldn't have.

That night I prayed, "Oh, Lord, thank you for running interference for me, and causing the salesman to show us the papers on the oriental rug. Thank you for the wisdom you have given Paul and for his spiritual leadership in our home. I am so blessed."

2

What Would You Have Said—

When the Officer in the Bank Thought God Had Forgotten Her?

Marja

I was surprised to see Marja, one of the officers of the bank, standing in line. She was waiting to get to the teller's window like the rest of the customers. I teased her a bit and asked her why such an important person had to take her turn to be waited on. "Why don't you go right up to the window," I suggested. "After all your time is valuable."

"Our customers' time is valuable too. I don't want to take advantage of them."

I liked this woman right away. *What an attitude,* I thought.

I was rather excited that day. My friends Ruth and Neil Duff had just had an autographing party for me. I had a number of checks in my hand ready to be deposited. Marja noticed and smiled.

"These checks will help pay for my new word process. reams of paper I use, and the cost of having photocopies made."

"The word processor must be a great help to you," she commented. "What is the name of your book?"

"What Do You Say When . . ."

"That's an interesting title. What's it about?"

"It's stories about people I've met who don't know how to be in the family of God. I tell them what God's requirements are. The Bible is my authority, since that's the Word of God—not my church nor my opinions."

"Where can I get a copy?" she asked.

"It won't be in the bookstores for another two weeks but the publisher sent me some copies. I have them in my car."

"Would you be willing to sell me a copy?"

"I'd be happy to," I replied.

"Do you suppose I could have two? I'd like to send one to my father."

I went to the car and brought back the books. "The next time I see you," I said," I'd appreciate it if you would give me an appraisal of the book. Let me know what you think of the message in it."

"Okay, I promise."

At the end of the week I had occasion to return to the bank. When I saw Marja, I walked up to her desk and asked, "Have you had a chance to browse through my book yet?"

"Both my husband and I have read it. The book has revolutionized our lives. I'll tell you about it if I get a chance the next time you come in," she answered as a customer approached her.

I saw her a week later. She motioned for me to come and sit down next to her desk. "Let me tell you what happened," she said in an excited tone of voice. "A few weeks ago, I was feeling very discouraged and very much alone. My husband, Ron, who is a diabetic, had been suffering

rated foot for almost three years. He has gone
[...]octors but his foot would not heal. He has expe-
[...]y ups and downs with fevers and at times seri-
[...]ns. The best the doctors could do was to keep
the foot from being amputated. I was very upset, and
began to ask, 'What next, Lord? Are you really there?'
When you came into the bank, I was at a very low point in
my life.

"After Ron and I read your book we realized other people had problems too, but God was always there. This
encouraged us to put our trust in God. We then realized
that for three years God had allowed Ron to keep his foot.
It caused us to give thanks. We now want him to be in control of our lives."

I wasn't absolutely sure if Marja knew what it meant to
trust Jesus Christ for her salvation, or if she understood
what it was all about.

I then asked her, "Marja, have you ever accepted Jesus
Christ as your personal Savior?"

"Oh, yes, I have, but I had allowed my problems to get
in the way and lost touch with God. I wondered if he really
cared about us, but now I know he does.

"We don't know what the future holds for us," she said,
"but we're leaving it all in his hands. We are sure God has
a purpose for allowing this to come into our lives. We
know him better now, and things are just fine."

Marja's personality has changed. She is radiant. The love
of Christ is evident in her life. One day she explained, "As I
continue to read the Word and increasingly trust the Lord,
everything seems to fall into place the way it should.
Things seem to work out much better when God is in control. In the back of my mind, I knew this to be true, but the
book brought it all into focus. I am so thankful for God's
perfect wisdom in bringing this into my life during a 'val-
ley' of my life. I hope I might spread the joy of the Lord by

sharing this with others. I need four more books if you can spare them," she said. "We have some friends we want to encourage." I was delighted with the change in her life.

About a week later as I was transacting some business, Marja came up to the teller's window and said, "When you're finished come over to my desk. I have some very good news to tell you."

She seemed so excited. I wondered what it was all about. "What's up?" I asked, as I sat down near her desk.

"Ron has an appointment at the University of Minnesota's Wound Healing Clinic. He is to try a new miracle cure, one with a ninety-five percent success rate so far. What they will do is extract blood from Ron, mix it with a new drug, and apply it on the affected area of his foot. The healing process then begins. We are to be there on Saturday. I'm so excited, I can hardly wait. God is so good. The best part, Nellie, is that both Ron and I decided to trust the Lord before we heard about the cure."

I had read about the cure in the newspaper that very day and had hoped it would be available for Ron. I was delighted when I heard an appointment had already been set up.

Marja and her husband left for Minnesota the following Saturday, and in less than a week Ron was allowed to come back home. The rest of the treatments were done by his local doctor. Marja showed me pictures of her husband's foot as the healing progressed. The first pictures looked like a large, raw, T-bone steak. The last ones were of a completely normal foot. Success was 100 percent.

The last time I saw Marja, she and her husband were preparing to drive to Washington State, where her parents live—their first vacation in several years. Then after they return Ron will be allowed to go back to work. It had been a long illness. I rejoiced with her at the goodness of the Lord in their lives.

Looking Back

Marja and Ron's attitude was not much different from the average Christian's. We get discouraged when we have problems. We pray and expect instant answers. Sometimes God does answer immediately, other times we must wait until his perfect work is done in us. It's a process that will bring rewards if we learn to trust him with our lives. I'm reminded of Romans 8:35, which says: "Who shall separate us from the love of Christ? Shall trouble or hardship or persecution or famine or nakedness or danger or sword?" Also verses 37–39:

No, in all these things we are more than conquerors through him who loved us. For I am convinced that neither death nor life, neither angels nor demons, neither the present nor the future, nor any powers, neither height nor depth nor anything else in all creation, will be able to separate us from the love of God that is in Christ Jesus our Lord.

3

What Would You Have Said—

If You Took One Step Forward and Found You Were Taking Two Steps Backward?

Florence

"I've got so much to do today, I barely know where to start," I remarked to my husband.

"Make a list and then cross off each item as you complete it," he said.

I knew what his answer would be. He's an engineer and always well organized; but he's also very patient and generally goes along with my strange ways. He knows I'll eventually learn.

"What I really wanted to do first was give my hair a good treatment. I was sure I had some conditioner left but I can't find it. I'll have to go to the drugstore and get some. I'll never get anything done at this rate," I complained.

As usual, Paul came to my rescue. "Let me help you look," he said. "I know it's hard to find things around here. Being in Florida part of the year can pose a problem at times. You may have left it in Michigan."

We both looked in the usual places without success.

On the way to the store I began planning my day. I had some thoughts in my head that needed to be transferred to paper. I needed to make a tape. The house needed touching up, and then there was the banquet in the evening. I wondered if I would ever get these things done.

When I arrived at the drug store I discovered it wouldn't be open for another half hour. There I go spinning my wheels again. *Why didn't I check on the time the store opened*, I thought.

Feeling utterly frustrated, I decided to wait. I'd only waste more time if I returned later.

While I stood *patiently* waiting, a woman walked up and asked, "isn't the store open yet?"

"No," I answered, "not until nine o'clock."

"This town!" she said in a disgusted voice. "Things take forever to get going."

"Where are you from?" I asked.

"Actually I've lived here for twenty-two years, but I'm from Bloomfield Hills, Michigan."

"That's interesting. I'm from Birmingham."

We discovered we lived only a few miles apart.

"Are you planning to move to Florida?" she asked.

"Not for a while. It's a hard decision to make. My son and his family live about eighty miles from us. We get to see them oftener when we are in Michigan. And we attend the church where I was raised. We get excellent Bible teaching, which means a lot to me. It's really the only authority we have for our belief in God."

"What is the name of your church?" she asked.

"Highland Park Baptist. It's in Southfield. Did you attend church when you lived in Michigan?" I asked.

"Yes, I attended a Presbyterian church," she said.

"Well, whether it's Baptist or Presbyterian, as long as the Bible is the authority, it's pretty safe."

She made no comment but I sensed she wasn't sure about what I had just said.

"You know," I said, "I meet people all over who don't know how to be in the family of God. I love to tell them what the Bible has to say about that. In fact I just recently wrote a book about people I have met and shared the gospel with. I got acquainted with a woman in a swimming pool who confided in me that she didn't know how to pray. She needed to talk to God but didn't know how. Another young woman was suffering from guilt and needed God's forgiveness. Many people are looking for answers to life."

"What is the name of your book?" she asked. "I need to get it right away."

"Why do you need to get it right away?" I asked.

"Because yesterday my sister was diagnosed as having terminal cancer. She doesn't know it yet. Her husband died a couple of years ago. He was an atheist, and my sister hasn't gone to church for years. I need to read that book to her."

"I have some books in the car. I'll go and get you one."

Just then the store opened. "I'll go and order my prescription. I'll be at the back of the store," she said.

When I returned, I heard the pharmacist say, "Your prescription will be ready in about twenty minutes."

"Let's sit down and talk while you're waiting," I suggested.

"Can you afford the time?" she asked. (I had told her about my busy schedule for the day.)

"I'll take the time," I answered.

Yes, I had plenty to do that day but I sensed that this woman had a need greater than any of mine. This was now my priority for the day.

"By the way, my name is Nellie. What is your name?" I asked.

"My name is Florence. I'm just wondering was it coincidence that we met today? I feel as though this was meant to be."

"I call these meetings 'God's divine appointments.' I believe he arranges them. Both of us were impatient about the store's opening so late, and yet God knew all about it. Rather amazing, isn't it?"

I discovered that even though Florence had attended church for many years, I didn't know if she had a relationship with Jesus Christ.

"Florence," I asked, "do you believe that you are a sinner and that God sent his Son Jesus Christ to die for you?"

"Yes, I know that I'm a sinner."

"Have you ever received Jesus Christ as your Savior from the guilt and penalty of sin?"

"No, I've never done that," she said with her head bowed.

"Would you like to do that?" I asked.

"Yes, I would." Then she turned to me and asked, "Will you help me pray?"

"When you pray, it isn't so much the words you say that are important, it's the attitude of your heart that God sees."

I helped her and she prayed. "Lord, I confess I'm a sinner. I've pretty much done things my own way. I want to receive Jesus as my Savior. I thank you for accepting me into your family and making me your child. Thank you for forgiving all my sin. Help me to walk in your way. In Jesus' name I pray, *Amen*."

"Florence, you are now in the family of God. In one way it was fairly simple. You acknowledged you were a sinner and received Jesus Christ as your Savior. Isn't it incredible when we realize the price Jesus Christ paid for our salvation? We deserved to die for our own sins, but Jesus opted to be our substitute. He paid the penalty, and we went scot-free. To me that is overwhelming."

I gave her a booklet that gives the basics of salvation so

she could understand what had transpired that day. I also suggested she start reading the Gospel of John.

I knew Florence would be completely tied up with the needs of her sister for the time being, so I didn't try to make arrangements for Bible studies. I felt we could keep in touch by phone.

I went home very excited about my experience. I could hardly wait to tell Paul. I was able to get my radio taping done, put my house in order, get some writing done, give my hair a good treatment, and had a wonderful time at the banquet that evening. Somehow everything fell into place!

The following morning I opened the door of the medicine cabinet in the bathroom. I couldn't believe my eyes. There it was, the bottle of conditioner I had been looking for! There were only a few items in the cabinet. How could I have missed it? How could Paul have missed it? He has eagle eyes. He doesn't miss a thing. I called my husband and said, "I want to show you something. You won't believe it. Look." I opened the door of the medicine cabinet and showed him the bottle of conditioner. "Why didn't we see that yesterday?" he asked. Then he added, "I guess the Lord wanted you to be at the drugstore so you could meet the need of a hungry heart." He gave me a big hug and said, "Isn't God amazing?"

I'm back in Michigan now, and while talking to Florence on the phone one day, she said, "I'll never get over the way God arranged for us to meet in front of the drugstore. It met a tremendous need in my life. Most of my time is taken up with caring for my sister but someone from hospice comes twice a week and that is a great help. Things are pretty much under control now."

Looking Back

Every once in a while I picture myself dashing to the store that March morning in Florida. I didn't want to waste

33

a minute. I was so concerned about the heavy schedule I had imposed on myself. I hadn't taken time to read or pray before I left. I figured I would do that while sitting under the hairdryer. Not a very good way to start the day. And yet in spite of myself, God used my frustrations to remind me that he, God, is in control of my life. I love it!

"Oh, the depth of the riches of the wisdom and knowledge of God!
How unsearchable his judgments, and his paths beyond tracing out!
Who has known the mind of the Lord? (Rom. 11:33, 34a).

4

What Would You Have Said—

If You Overheard Someone Talking About Your Friend?

Jim

"I couldn't help overhearing you talk about a friend of mine," I said, addressing the saleswoman.

She looked up and seemed a little surprised as she said, "Oh, you mean Jim Devine. He's the president of our company."

"Yes, I know," I answered. "We have a great deal of respect for him, not only for his accomplishments but for his integrity as a person."

"I couldn't ask for a better boss," she agreed. "He comes in the store every week. He's friendly and keeps tabs on what's going on. We appreciate that because it helps us feel secure. It's really a wonderful place to work."

"We have known Jim and his wife for several years," I

explained. "They are from our home state, Michigan. I'm glad you like him.

"There a reason why he's such a super guy, in case you didn't know," I confided, with a smile.

The clerk seemed interested in my statement and asked, "What is that?"

"Well, Jim's first allegiance is to the Lord whom he serves. His relationship to God affects his whole life."

"I knew it had to be something like that," she said. "It really does show. I'm a Christian too. I hope people can tell."

I then walked to the other side of the store. I couldn't believe my ears. It happened again. I heard one of the sales women talk to a distributor about the head of her company. So once again I said, "You are talking about my friend."

"You mean Jim Devine?"

"Yes."

"He's really a great guy. Nice to work for," the clerk agreed.

It worked before, I thought, *I'll try it again,* so I said, "There's a reason why he's such a nice guy."

The distributor looked surprised and asked, "Is it because he's German?"

"No," I laughed. Having been born in Norway, I teased a bit as I went on, "Now if he were a Norwegian, I might say it had something to do with it."

"Give me one more try," the distributor said. We were all having fun. "Is it because he has a terrific wife?"

"Though that is true, that is not the reason why he's such a great guy."

"Well then, what is the reason? It's got to be something very special."

"It is something special. You see, Jim has a personal relationship with Jesus Christ. It affects everything he does. He believes he's accountable to God for his actions. You see, he loves the Lord and his desire is to serve him."

"Wow, maybe he'll go easy on the girl who made that horrible error this morning."

"You must understand that just because he's a Christian and a very kind person, doesn't mean he'll accept poor work. He's responsible to his boss in the company too. He's no softy, I can tell you that. But I'll guarantee, he'll be fair," I said.

"Very interesting," he mused.

"By the way," I asked, "what is your relationship as far as God is concerned? Do you mind telling me?"

"I really don't bother about God. I don't need him. I'm a good person. I really am."

"How can anyone who doesn't bother about God—the One who created the universe—the sun, moon, and stars, water to drink, and food to eat—be good? How can a person who is ungrateful be good?"

"Well, I really don't need God. Religion is not for me."

"We all have a need to have our sins forgiven," I said.

"But I don't have any sin that needs forgiveness."

"Your greatest sin is ignoring God, leaving him out of your life, and rejecting Jesus Christ."

"I'm really not interested in religion, but I do like to hear you talk. I'm interested in your viewpoint."

"Since you're interested in my viewpoint, this is what I'll do. I'll just pray that God will give you a need. Maybe that will cause you to call on him."

"I don't think you should do that," he protested. It seemed to make him feel uneasy.

"Someday you'll have a need that only God can meet. You won't know how to reach him, since you're not in his family."

"I'll take my chances," he replied.

As I prepared to leave, I said, "You do have a right to choose. The Bible says that in Joshua 24:15: 'Choose for yourselves this day whom you will serve. . . .'"

"It looks like you've made your choice. Of course you have to live with the consequences," I stated. "I suppose

I've talked enough. I really didn't mean to give you a hard time."

"I'm really not interested, but I do like to hear you talk," he said again.

That made me chuckle. "You're not interested, but you want me to keep talking?

"Yeah, I'm interested in your viewpoint."

It sounded like we were going around in circles. I figured that he was afraid to face the truth about his eternal destiny. He covered up by telling me that he was okay, that he was actually a good person.

I talked a little longer. I told him that Jesus Christ was the only real good person, the only perfect one; that we can't even pray directly to God because we are sinners. But we can come through Jesus Christ.

"Well, I'm not sure about that."

I asked him what his name was so that I could tell my friend Jim that we had had a good talk. He readily told me. Then he said, "If you'll wait here I'll go out in the car and get you a sample of our product. He didn't seem a bit offended about our conversation. In fact he said, "I enjoyed talking to you."

I'm glad I didn't turn him off. I prayed that the Spirit of God would remind him of the things we talked about.

Jim did meet this young man whose name was Barry and talked to him about our conversation.

At least this distributor knew what made my friend Jim so kind and that the reason he was so different was because he serves the true and living God. I pray he will never forget this incident in his life and that someday he will discover the joy of knowing Jesus Christ as his own personal Savior.

Looking Back

Jim may not have realized it, but he had a good reputation and testimony for the Lord in the workplace. He was not just a Sunday Christian. Having a good reputation is part of the Christian's responsibility. We are the only Bible some people read. I also think of Psalm 139:2–4 in which we are reminded:

> You know when I sit and when I rise;
> you perceive my thoughts from afar;
> You discern my going out and my lying down;
> you are familiar with all my ways.
> Before a word is on my tongue
> you know it completely, O LORD.

The world is full of people who are taking their chances. "I'll live life to the full," they say. "I'll take my chances about God. He just doesn't fit into my scheme of things."

I'm glad Jim didn't let success go to his head. He's a good role model for his employees because he is first of all accountable to God.

Jim's Christian training was not in his home, since he's only known the Lord thirteen years. But from the time he accepted Christ as his Savior, he has been sitting under good Bible teaching. According to his wife, he has the ability to receive the Word and act on it immediately. I loved it when she told me that Jim is so uncomplicated. It reminded me of Jesus when he said to Nathanael that he was a man without guile (*see* John 1:47). In other words there is nothing fake about him.

I wondered why so many of the employees seemed to know about Jim. I asked his wife about that. She told me that though he is president of his company, he is more like a "hands-on manager." He believes in visiting his stores on a regular basis. He believes in getting to know the people that work for him in a personal way. He is not aloof just because he is the president.

I had a chance to share Christ with one of his vendors. I may never see him again but I know that if Barry has any questions, he'll know where to get his answers.

As Christians, we are on God's team. One sows, someone else waters but only God can give the increase.

5

What Would You Have Said—

If the Real Estate Woman Ignored You and Addressed Only Your Husband?

Patricia

Paul and I were house hunting. We had seen some townhouses advertised in the paper and decided to check them out. We wanted to see if they were as nice as the artist's sketch.

I was impressed with the beauty of the saleswoman assigned to us. Her dark hair and eyes contrasted with her flawless light skin. Her perfect figure caused me to admire her.

I was not impressed, however, with the wiggle in her hips and shoulders when she walked. And I was not impressed when she didn't even look at me but turned to my husband and in a sultry voice asked, "And how are you today?"

I looked at Paul to get his reaction. He gave me a know-ing smile. I knew he understood. "I think I'd better hang onto you," I whispered. His eyes twinkled as he smiled.

The first model we entered looked bright and cheerful. We liked the size of the rooms. Patricia, our salesperson then asked, "Do you have any specific need as far as a home is concerned?" she asked.

"Well, yes. My wife needs a place for her word proces-sor. She is doing some writing. A small den or alcove would do just fine."

"Oh," she said turning to me, "what do you write about?"

"I write about people who are searching for the meaning of life. Many of them have had success in the world as far as money and careers are concerned. After achieving what they went after, there is still a longing for something better. They don't find it satisfying or fulfilling. Others thought they would find fulfillment in marriage, but something was missing. I tell them about Jesus Christ, who came to give them abundant life—the Bible being my authority. I tell them what God's requirements are. I don't tell them the beliefs of a particular church or my opinion. I tell them what the Bible says since that is God's Word."

"That sounds great," she said. "Have you ever heard of Bibletown?"

"Why, yes, we are associate members. We spend our winters here in Florida and are very active in that church," I said.

"My daughter attends their school," she said. "Boca Raton Christian School. I would work my fingers to the bone so she can attend. It's really a wonderful school."

"Where do you attend church?" I asked.

She hesitated for a moment and then said, "I don't attend church." She sounded apologetic.

"That surprises me," I said. "Do you mean to tell me that you send your daughter to school to get a Christian education and yet you don't attend church at all?"

"It wouldn't do any good," she answered.

"Why? I asked.

"My priest said that when I die, I will go straight to hell."*

"Why?"

"Because of my great sin," she answered.

"But that's why Jesus Christ died—for your great sin and mine."

She shook her head in bewilderment and seemed to dismiss the subject for the time being.

We looked at a few more models and then headed back to the office.

Her mind must have been on our previous conversation because on the way back she said, "Part of my daughter's homework is to memorize Scripture. I'm learning some of the verses too. I'm also reading the Book of Proverbs. It's great. I get a lot out of it."

How can I go back to Michigan tomorrow without telling her how she can know Jesus Christ as her personal Savior? I thought.

When we arrived at the office I turned to Patricia and asked, "Do you have five minutes to spare? I would like to tell you why Jesus Christ died on the cross and how you can have your sins forgiven."

"Yes, I can take a few minutes."

"Patricia, I don't know what your particular sin is but Jesus Christ died on the cross for that sin. He paid the ultimate penalty. In fact the Bible says in Romans 5:8 that 'God demonstrates his own love for us in this: While we were still sinners, Christ died for us.' The Bible also says in Romans 3:23: 'for all have sinned and fall short of the glory of God.' There isn't a person in the world that has met God's standards. But the good news is that God will accept

*I recognize that not all priests agree with this extreme position, but Patricia's priest was emphatic about her punishment.

you into his family if you confess that you are a sinner and need his son, Jesus Christ to be your personal Savior. You must ask Jesus to be Lord of your life."

She seemed to hang on to every word I said.

"Just think, he who knew no sin became sin for you and for me. We deserved to die but he chose to become our substitute.

"You must have been living a miserable existence, thinking you were doomed to hell," I said.

"Well, even though the priest said I was going straight to hell when I die, I determined in my heart that my daughter would have a chance. That is why I'm sending her to a Christian school."

"You don't have to go to hell, Patricia. Jesus said, 'I have come that they may have life, and have it to the full' (John 10:10). He wants that for you. He wants you to trust him and believe everything he says. He also said, 'I am the way . . .'"

Before I could finish she interrupted and said, " '. . . the truth and the life. No one comes to the Father except through me.' That's one of my daughter's memory verses. I learned it too."

"That's just great," I was excited. *Maybe there's a chance for Patricia,* I thought.

"We haven't talked very long," I said, "but would you be ready and willing even now to confess to God that you are a sinner, and ask Jesus Christ to be your Savior and Lord?"

"Oh, yes, if there's a chance for me, I would," she said as her voice broke.

She bowed her head ready to pray when the telephone rang. It was the front office. "We need you at the desk immediately," her boss said.

"I'll be there in two minutes," she said. She wasn't going to let this opportunity go by. She prayed, "Dear heavenly Father, I know I have sinned against you. I've gone my own independent way. Thank you for sending your Son to die on the cross for my sins. I now receive Jesus Christ as my Savior and Lord. I want you to take charge of my life. Thank you for making me a member of your family. In Jesus' name I pray . . . *Amen.*"

When she raised her head, I noticed tears in her eyes but her face was radiant. What a special moment that was. I gave her a hug. After all, we were now sisters in the Lord.

We headed for the front office. Patricia went directly to my husband and said, "I want you to know I just invited Jesus Christ into my life. I'm now a member of his family."

Looking Back

If Patricia had not meant business with the Lord, she could have used that telephone call from the front office as an excuse to leave. But she proved that God's offer of salvation came first, regardless of the cost.

In a vague way Patricia knew that Jesus died on the cross for the sins of mankind, but since she had apparently been told that her sin was unforgivable, she felt she didn't have a chance with God.

I judged her mannerisms at the beginning. I didn't see her aching heart. God says that's what we do as humans. ". . . Man looks on the outward appearance but the LORD looks at the heart" (1 Sam. 16:7). I'm glad God softened my heart toward her and helped me to see her great need. I'm also glad that God allowed me to be the instrument to lead her to Christ.

It was eight months before I saw Patricia again. One of the first things she told me was, "God has met my needs in ways I never dreamed possible. It's unbelievable."

"We have a great God, don't we?" I responded.

"Besides my other problems, I've also been divorced," she said. "How does God view divorce?"

"God hates divorce. It was his plan from the beginning that families stay together. Divorce creates a lot of problems. It divides families, fosters hatred, hurts children, and robs us of peace. Jesus came to bring peace. As much as is in us he wants us to live in peace. Matthew 19:8 says that in the law of Moses, God permitted divorce because of the hardness of their hearts. We have to live with our mistakes but divorce is not the unforgivable sin," I said.

She needed to tell me her story. "I was very young when I married. My parents didn't approve. Perhaps they could see things I wasn't aware of. I didn't listen to them. I know I broke their hearts. I went ahead and married. I have so many regrets.

"My former husband is much older than I am and is from another country. Everything was great at the beginning, but then after a while he began to stay away, days at a time. I was left confused and hurt. He finally left me for other women. He has given no financial support for me and my two children. I was devastated. And I was already hurting because my priest told me I would go straight to hell when I die. I'm so glad God has forgiven my sin and I'm in his family. Since I accepted Christ as my Savior, he has met all of my needs. God has provided. I'm ever so grateful."

"Just think of the blessing your little girl has been in your life," I said.

"She's incredible. She's only nine years old and every semester she has received an award for her Bible memorization. I'm so proud of her. She's taught me a lot. Do you know that she would come home from school and ask, 'Mom, have you accepted Christ yet?' I had to say no because I figured it wouldn't do me any good."

"I'm glad I had a part in leading you to Christ, but your daughter sowed the seed and got you into the Scriptures. Let me tell you how Jesus prayed once. 'I praise you Father, Lord of heaven and earth, because you have hidden these things from the wise and learned, and revealed them to little children. Yes, Father, for this was your good pleasure' (Matt. 11:25, 26). God uses everyone who is available to him, even little children."

46

What Would You Have Said—

When a Woman Was Dropped Off at the Hospital and Faced Surgery Alone?

Betty

If I could get out of the car and walk straight into the operating room, it wouldn't be so bad. I couldn't convince my doctor that it was a good idea. It's the waiting around that gets to me. So, like an obedient child, I went through the proper procedures.

My husband parked the car and met me in the admitting room. I tried to relax, but all I could think of was my pending operation.

The woman sitting across the room from me seemed to be in a worse condition than I. Her nervousness was more obvious than mine. At least I thought so.

47

"I guess this isn't your favorite place either," I commented. We laughed, and I think it helped both of us.

"Are you waiting for your husband?" I asked.

"No, I don't expect to see him anymore."

I was puzzled. It must have shown on my face because she then said, "I'm to have a cancer operation. My husband can't handle it, so he said he'd drop me off at the hospital, and that would be the end of it for us."

I was flabbergasted. "You mean he's leaving you?" I asked.

She put her head in her hands and began to weep. "That's what he said."

(God certainly knew how to get my attention away from myself!)

"Would you like me to come and see you after we get settled in our rooms?"

"That would mean a lot to me," she said. "Maybe we could talk and I won't feel quite so alone."

I began to count my blessings and asked God to show me how to help this forsaken woman.

I soon discovered that my new friend, Betty, had a room just a few doors from mine. I believe that it was the Lord's provision. It made it so convenient for me to visit her.

After the nurses and interns had taken their blood samples and asked the proper questions, I walked down the hall to her room.

"I wondered if you would really come," she said. "Since your husband is with you, I didn't know. I thought you might have changed your mind. He seems so nice. You are so lucky," she said wistfully.

"Yes, God has blessed me with a good husband, and I certainly am thankful."

We chatted for a while about our operations—both of us anxious to have them over. Then she told me about her little boy. A neighbor was keeping him for a few days.

"He's too young to visit me here in the hospital, but if

things go well, I will at least have him to go home to. He's a great comfort to me." She didn't complain, just stated the facts about her situation. It was hard for her to talk about her husband, so I didn't probe.

"Do you have a church family at all?" I asked. "What I really mean is do you attend church anyplace?"

"No, I haven't attended in years. My husband didn't care to go, so I stayed home with him. I did try to please him. I just didn't do a good job." She then turned to look at me and said, "I'm so glad you came. I really don't expect to have any visitors while I'm here. It's not fun being alone."

"I've put my trust in Jesus Christ," I said, "because he promised to never leave us nor forsake us. If you will put your trust in him and receive him as your Savior, he'll stay close by. You will never be alone. By the way, I brought a book along I'd like you to have. I think you'll enjoy reading it, and I believe it will help you.

"If you will allow me, I'd like to share my family with you. I have three children, and they plan to visit me. My oldest daughter, Karen, will be returning to Wheaton College soon but you'll get to meet her. Tim will be starting at Michigan State, and Greta is still in high school. In a few days, if you're feeling up to it, my husband will check on you to see if you would like some company. I know you'll love them, and I'm sure they'll love you too," I said.

The next few days were just plain rotten for me. I felt miserable. I did my share of moaning and groaning and waited for the nurse to get me some pain pills. But the pain soon passed. My operation was major but not earth shattering. I began to feel better and wondered how my new friend was. I discovered that she had had a rough time but the doctors felt they had gotten all the cancer. The future looked brighter for her.

When the children heard that Betty's husband had left her they were sad.

"How could he leave his wife when she needed him so

desperately?" my daughter Karen asked. "How can a husband be so cruel? I know Daddy would never do that."

"Not everyone is blessed with a Christian husband and father," I replied. "Knowing Jesus Christ makes all the difference in the world."

The children were so used to the kindness of their father that they found this situation incredible.

They took some of the flowers I had received from my friends and brought them to her. She couldn't get over their loving ways. I was proud of them.

My hospital stay lasted about ten days, and I spent the next few weeks recuperating. Then it was time to outfit the children for school. Because of the busyness of life, I lost track of my new friend.

At Christmastime, two years later, I received a card. I couldn't decipher the name of the sender. And because there was no return address on the envelope, I had no idea where it came from. The following Christmas I received another card. It was again difficult to read the name. This time I called the telephone operator and told her my dilemma. "Would you be willing to help me decipher a name?" We tried several combinations, and finally she said, "Let me try this number." I couldn't believe a telephone operator would be so patient. She must have been sent by the Lord. When the phone rang and the woman answered, I told her my name and that I had received a Christmas card two years in a row. "I'm embarrassed to say that I don't recognize the name."

"Don't you remember me? You led me to Christ in the hospital through the book you gave me that explained how I could be in God's family. I accepted Christ as my Savior, and my son and I now attend church regularly. We even help at the church. We take care of the flower beds around the church. We love it."

Amazing, I thought. "I would love to see you. Would you be able to come and have lunch at my home? I want you to

50

meet some of my Christian friends. I want them to share in the goodness of God. I didn't feel that I had done a good job in sharing the gospel with you, but God overrruled and used the book I gave you."

"It was the love you and your family showed me that made me want what you had. I have discovered for myself that it's Jesus Christ who makes the difference."

She came for lunch. It was exciting to see my Christian friends seated around the dining-room table getting acquainted with this new member of the family of God. It was a great day of rejoicing.

"You told me something important that has stayed with me. It has been a great comfort. You said that God would never leave me nor forsake me. I have found it to be so true. I now have wonderful security in him."

Looking Back

Going to the hospital and having surgery is never fun—but God can even use an unpleasant experience to bring glory to his name. I gave her a book to read. I had no idea how effective it would be—but God used it.

I'm glad I responded to the nudge God gave me to minister to someone who had a greater need than my own.

Being an effective witness takes time and experience. If we give God what we have, he multiplies it and brings blessing out of the small things in life—like the little boy with the loaves and the fishes. It has been said before, "Little is much when God is in it." Let's give God what we have and see what he will do with it.

What Would You Have Said—

When You Were Very Busy and a Salesman Called, Wanting to Keep You on the Line?

Telemarketing

Everything seemed to go well that morning. The feeling of always being behind was fast fading away. I was finally catching up on my household chores. I had finished the laundry and even polished some company silver. *I'm on top of things this morning,* I thought.

I had just settled down to do some writing when the telephone rang. Since my husband wasn't home, I felt compelled to answer it. It might be an important call.

"Hello," the intruder said, "Are you Mrs. Pickard?"

"Yes, that's my name."

"How are you feeling today?"

"Just fine, thank you."

"Haven't we been having beautiful weather lately? And isn't it a beautiful day?"

I felt an attack of impatience coming on. It seemed as though my friends and I had been bombarded with solicitors calling anytime of day and night. I knew this was another such call. I wanted to hang up. A battle was going on, inside me. One part of me said, "Be polite Nellie; he's only doing his job." The other part said, "Why doesn't he get a job that doesn't bother people?"

The better part of me finally won out, so I said as politely as was humanly possible, "I really don't have much time to chat this morning. I'm working on a manuscript. I would appreciate it if you would tell me the purpose of your call."

"I'm offering you a wonderful opportunity. We can give you a complete food service, guaranteeing you the best nutrition available anywhere. We bring everything right to the house."

"Thank you, but we won't need it," I answered.

"But nutritionally, it's the best."

"Thank you so much. My sister is a nutritionist, and she gives me all the help I need." I didn't add "when she can get me to listen to her advice."

"Before you hang up," he said, "Would you mind telling me what you're writing about?"

"Strange you should ask. That is something I always have time to talk about. I write about people with whom I have shared God's requirements to be in his family, the Bible being my authority."

"Now I find that very interesting," he said. "I just recently accepted Jesus as my Savior. You are the third person this week that has mentioned something about God. In fact, a man said to me just yesterday 'Something good is going to happen to you today.' And it did."

"What happened?" I asked.

"I won the lottery."

I was totally unprepared for that answer. "Did you say you have accepted Jesus Christ as your Savior?" I asked.

"Yes, I have."

"Then what in the world are you doing playing the lottery?"

There was dead silence, then he said sheepishly, "I think I need a little help along that line."

"I think you do, too. Now that you've won some money are your plans to spend more and more money on the lottery, hoping to win the big one?"

"Yeah, I guess that's what I was hoping for," he answered.

"Don't you realize that all your energy, time, and thoughts are going to be consumed with winning more and more money? Now that you have accepted Christ as your Savior, don't you think you should be spending time reading the Bible? If you do that, then you will get to know God better. That is more exciting than anything money can buy. Don't you agree?"

"I see what you mean. I was pretty excited about my winnings. I guess God meant for me to talk to you today. Strange that your phone number was on my list of calls for today."

"Let me give you a good suggestion. Start reading the Gospel of John. Read a little each day, think about what you've read during the day. It will change your entire outlook on life. It will add sparkle to your life. After all the Bible is God's letter to us. If we seek him first he will add the things we need in life."

"Thanks again," he said before he hung up.

I put the phone back on the hook. Then I stood in the middle of the room and laughed at myself and thought, *I can't believe what just happened*. Then I prayed, "Thank you, Lord, for helping me overcome my frustration at the salesman on the telephone. I could have muffed it but you turned my weakness into a blessing. You are great and deserve all my praise. Help me never to forget that I'm your ambassador."

Looking Back

I'm grateful for the restraining force of the Holy Spirit. I almost gave in to my human impulses to hang up the phone on the troublesome caller. What caused me to change my mind? It was the gentle nudge of the Spirit of God within me. He reminded me that I had made a commitment to be available to God. I needed that. I so easily forget.

I almost missed an opportunity to encourage a brother in Christ. I knew only two things about the caller. He had just accepted Jesus Christ as his Savior and he had won the lottery a few days previously. These two things are opposed to each other. They are two different mind-sets. The first one longs to know God better. The second yearns to fulfill the fleshly desire for more and more things. As it says in Matthew 6:33, 34:

"But seek first his kingdom and his righteousness, and all these things will be given to you as well. Therefore do not worry about tomorrow, for tomorrow will worry about itself. Each day has enough trouble of its own."

Becoming a believer in Jesus Christ is just the first step. Maturing in the Christian life takes one step after another. There is much a new believer doesn't know. This man needs to be discipled. He needs to get into the Word on a daily basis, so that he will know what the will of God is for his life. Then he will be able to distinguish between the devil's wiles and God's best for his life.

Since the caller was a man, I did not want to go beyond what I felt was proper. I prayed for him. I prayed that God would send someone alongside him to encourage him in the faith and in the study of God's Word.

I often put a P.S. on my letters, and I think this episode needs a P.S.

I thought I had finished this chapter but decided to add something that just happened.

I went to pick up a few needed items at the store. While waiting to pay my bill, I noticed the woman in front of me hesitate, then she picked up one of those trashy newspapers available at the counter. She turned around and gave me a strange smile. It was as though she was apologizing, or that she had been caught in the act of doing something wrong. *Interesting,* I thought.

The headlines said, "Lucy was in contact with the dead before she died."

"You don't believe that do you?" I asked.

"Naw, I didn't buy this paper for myself. It's for my mom. What else is there for a sixty-seven year old woman to do? She gets a big kick out of it."

"Sixty-seven! Mmm, that *is* old," I said as I chuckled to myself. "I would think she'd enjoy reading the Bible. That's where you find out about life after death."

"Oh, my mother reads the Bible, and I do, too."

"I'm surprised to hear that. The things you read in that paper and the things you read in the Bible are opposed to each other. The Bible says in Deuteronomy 18 that trying to consult the dead is a detestable thing in God's sight."

Because the young lady in front of me didn't seem to object to my talking, (in fact she appeared to agree), I continued. "Reading the Bible and reading those sensational newspapers are a part of two opposite lifestyles. They just don't go together. Then I said with a smile and in a teasing voice, "How about telling your mom about our conversation? And don't forget to remind her of Deuteronomy 18."

"I'm going to do that," she said. "Have a good day, and it was nice chatting with you."

Romans 16:19 says: ". . . be wise about what is good, and innocent about what is evil." Philippians 4:8 says, "Finally, brothers, whatever is true, whatever is noble, whatever is right, whatever is pure, whatever is lovely, whatever is admirable—if anything is excellent or praiseworthy—think about such things." And as Paul continues, "Put these things into practice" (*see* v. 9).

In one day I talked to two people with the same problem. Both were toying with the devil's tools. Not knowing them personally I had no idea in which stage of growth they were. It did make me realize how important it is for Christians to be discipled and to be encouraged not only to read God's Word but also to obey it.

I continually pray that God will help me to love what he loves and hate what he hates. I want to be his faithful servant.

What Would You Have Said—

When One of the Class Members Told You Her Husband Was Having an Affair with Their Neighbor?

Caroline

"I hope Caroline shows up in class today," Joanne said, "I've called and invited her several times. Even though she says our Bible study is exactly what she needs, I sense a reluctance on her part to make a commitment to come. I'm not sure what her problem is."

"Do you think she's shy? Maybe she doesn't like coming by herself," I suggested.

"I'm not sure. I've offered to pick her up, but she doesn't want me to go out of my way. I think I'll call one of our mutual friends and invite her to our class. They live near each other. Maybe that will give her an incentive to come."

Joanne was a real asset in our Bible class. She brought several unbelievers during the course of the year. She would introduce me to her friends and leave. I often laughed to myself. I wonder if Joanne is thinking, *Now I've done my part by inviting my friends. Here, it's up to you to lead them to Christ.*

As time went on, I realized how beautifully the body of Christ worked together. Everyone did his/her part.

Joanne didn't give up on Caroline and was finally rewarded by seeing her friend come to class.

I sensed Caroline's insecurity at first but the women were so loving and friendly that it wasn't long before she felt a part of the group.

During our discussion time one day, Caroline said, "I had wanted to come to this Bible study for a long time but I have a problem: I'm fearful of leaving the house. I don't like to be in a car alone either. I wasn't sure if I'd be able to handle being in a group, but my desire and need to study the Bible helped me to overcome my fear. I finally got the courage to come and I'm glad I'm here. I do need your prayers though."

I was surprised and pleased that she was so honest and open with the class. She was becoming more outgoing, and I was glad she was willing to take part in class prayer requests. Caroline wanted help and wasn't afraid to ask. I found her to be a most delightful person. *There's hope for her,* I thought.

She confided in me later that her problem was called *agoraphobia* (a dreadful fear of being alone in open or public places). Even though Caroline was tense at first, little by little she began to relax.

From the start I could see this new member of the class eating up the Scriptures. I wanted to talk to her about her personal relationship with Jesus Christ but didn't want to rush her. I wanted her to feel secure in the group first.

I had made a point of including the plan of salvation in

our lesson. I felt when I did approach her about her relationship to Jesus Christ she would have had time to think it through and make a decision.

Since this was a neighborhood Bible study the women attending were from various backgrounds and denominations. We decided from the beginning that we would not pick at the differences in our churches' beliefs but our authority would be the Scriptures.

"Feel free to ask questions," I said, "but the answers will come from the Bible. After all it is the Word of God."

Everyone agreed but, once in a while someone would say, "But our church believes. . . ."

"Let's see what the Bible has to say about it," I replied. "After all that's God's Word, and we did agree from the start that it would be our authority."

The women who were knowledgeable in the Scripture would help by looking up the answers in their concordances. The ones who weren't familiar with the Bible soon learned where to find the answers.

I recently met a woman who had been in our class several years ago. She confided in me that she used to be confused about some of the traditions in her church. "I've learned where to find my answers. I go directly to the source of truth now. I really enjoy studying the Bible."

I was delighted. That's what Bible studies are all about—to teach the women where to go for their source of truth.

One day someone brought some religious material from Unity. It was a daily reading booklet.

"This has a lot of good things in it," the woman said. "I need to know if it's according to the Bible. What do you know about it, Nellie?"

"I do know that Unity does not believe Jesus is God," I said. We have just been studying the Book of John and we have seen convincing proof that Jesus is indeed God in the flesh."

"Let's look at a couple of verses in the first chapter of John," I suggested. "The answer is in the very first verse. 'In the beginning was the Word, and the Word was with God, and the Word was God.' It goes on to say, 'He was with God in the beginning. Through him all things were made; without him nothing was made that has been made.' Lets skip down to the fourteenth verse. 'The Word became flesh and lived for a while among us. We have seen his glory, the glory of the one and only Son, who came from the Father, full of grace and truth.'

"If we had no other evidence in the Bible but the Book of John," I said, "we have enough proof that Jesus is God in the flesh. Anything contrary to God's Word is a false religion. I would not continue reading that booklet."

"Are you sure they don't believe Jesus is God?" she asked. "They don't say anything about that in their literature. Everything in this booklet sounds so right. It makes me feel good."

"We live by faith in Jesus Christ, not by our feelings," I said.

"I tell you what I'll do. I'll call Unity and ask them, and then I'll tell you exactly what they say."

The next week I came with my answer. "I called Unity Temple. I asked the woman who answered the phone, 'Does Unity believe Jesus is God in the flesh?'

"The woman hemmed and hawed. She had a hard time answering. Finally she said, 'I don't know what to say but we believe God is within you. We don't worship anything outside ourselves.'"

"Do you believe we are born sinners?" I asked.

"No, we believe we are born perfect," she said.

"Then why did Jesus Christ have to die on the cross?" I asked.

"You are taking isolated verses out of the Bible," was her answer.

"I perceive that you don't know the Scriptures at all," I

said. Our Bible class is studying the Book of John in the New Testament. It is full of evidences of God's love for us by sending his Son, Jesus Christ, to die in our place and for our sins."

The woman insisted that she believed the Bible. I very kindly suggested she start reading in the Book of John."

The class accepted my report and decided they wanted to be better Bible students.

After we had finished our lesson, Caroline shyly asked, "Could you come to my home and have lunch with me next week? I have a lot of questions that have been piling up in my mind. I don't feel free to ask them in class. I hope you can come."

I had been waiting for this opportunity. I didn't have to ask to talk to her. She asked me. *A perfect situation*, I thought. I sensed she was ready to apply the truth she had been hearing.

"I would love to come for lunch," I said.

Caroline was excited as she greeted me at the door. I had no sooner entered when she said, "My husband left instructions for me to bake something special for you. He said to be sure the house was in spick-and-span condition when you come. 'After all, it is your Bible teacher.'"

"It's interesting," she went on, "my husband was very fussy about the house being in good order. It was very important to him because my Bible teacher was coming. But his life is anything *but* orderly."

There was a quiver in Caroline's voice as she said, "I've discovered that my husband has been unfaithful. I don't know what to do."

"Are you sure about that?" I asked.

"Oh, yes. It's one of the neighbor women," she replied. They jog together every morning and then end up at her house. I've known about it for some time. My friend Jane says I should throw him out of the house, but I love him and he's my children's father. What do you think?"

"Have you confronted your husband or the woman about it?" I asked.

"No, I'm not sure how to do that," she answered.

"Before we try to solve your problem," I said, "let's pray about it. But before we pray, I need to ask you if you have ever asked Jesus Christ into your life to be your Savior and Lord?"

"Actually that's why I invited you to come over today," she said. "You probably don't know it but my religious background is Christian Science. From what I learned in class it isn't very different from Unity. I know they don't believe Jesus is God in the flesh. Also we have been taught that we don't sin because we're born perfect. I never did believe that. I see the evidences of sin all around me. What my husband is doing is sin. I know I sin and my children sin. Now that I'm reading the Bible, I know that being born perfect isn't true. We're all sinners. Because of that I need Jesus Christ in my life. I need to be forgiven of my sin. I do want him as my Savior. Will you tell me how I can do that?"

Talk about picking ripe fruit—Caroline was ready. She understood what it was all about.

"All you have to do is to ask him. Jesus said ' . . . whoever comes to me I will never drive away' (John 6:37)."

"You mean I should bow my head and pray?"

"That's the way you talk to God," I said. "I'll help you. It isn't so much the words you say that are important. It's the attitude of your heart that God sees."

Caroline prayed and invited Jesus Christ into her life to be her Savior and Lord.

"Caroline, you can now talk to your Father in heaven and tell him all your needs. You can ask him for wisdom concerning your husband. He's promised in Philippians 4:19 to meet all your needs according to his riches in glory. There is another verse you should hang on to. It's Hebrews 4:16. 'Let us then approach the throne of grace with confidence, so that we may receive mercy and find grace to help us in our time of need.'"

We then thanked God for his mercy and grace and for making Caroline his very own child. We thanked him for the security we have in him because Jesus said: "Never will I leave you; never will I forsake you" (Heb. 13:5).

"Could you stay and have a cup of coffee and another brownie before you leave?" Caroline asked.

I had tasted her brownies earlier. "They're the best I've ever eaten. I can't resist. I'd love to stay."

As we began sipping our coffee, she asked, "Do you have any idea what I should do about my husband's unfaithfulness?"

"Let's stop and pray and ask God for his wisdom. He has promised that if anyone lacks wisdom we should ask him and he will give it to us [see James 1:5]. Now that you have put your trust in him, you have every right to ask him for help. In fact, he wants you to ask him."

We both prayed concerning the problem.

"I've waited long enough," she decided. "I think this woman has a hold on my husband. Perhaps I should write her a letter and tell her I know what's going on. She has a husband and family too. I wonder if she's willing to lose them?"

"What will you tell her?" I asked.

"I don't know but I'd like you to read the letter before I send it. I do want to be wise about it."

I prayed much for Caroline the following week, knowing she had a difficult task before her.

One day she called and asked if I'd stop over. She had finished the letter and wanted to read it to me.

The letter came right to the point. She told the woman that she knew what was going on between her and her husband.

"I can't handle it any longer," she wrote. "You are welcome to my husband but you can't have it both ways.

Make up your mind immediately, or I will be compelled to go to your husband and tell him what has been going on."

"Are you prepared for the consequences?" I asked.

"I have a feeling neither one of them are willing to give up their families. As I told her in the letter, they can't have it both ways."

Caroline mailed the letter, and then she gave her husband a copy. She told me later that he panicked. "Oh, you shouldn't have sent that letter," he said. "What if someone gets a hold of it?"

Caroline replied, "You should have thought of that before you got involved." She told me later, "It's amazing how calm I was. I just stated the facts."

"I am so sorry," he said, "It never should have happened. I really don't love her. It's you I love. I will talk to her right away."

Within a few days the problem was resolved. The woman involved also panicked. She was concerned about losing her family, too. They agreed to stop their foolishness immediately.

"I have forgiven my husband," Caroline said, "but he is having a hard time forgiving himself. I know he loves me and I know he loves the children. I want to be a good wife to him. I'm trying to get him to come to church with me. He needs help with the guilt he's carrying around. He needs to know that not only have I forgiven him, but God is willing to forgive him, too. I know this will take place when he invites Jesus Christ into his life."

Looking Back

From Caroline we can all learn a lesson of forgiveness. I've noticed there is no bitterness in her heart. Her desire is to grow in the Lord and go on with her life. She is praying that her husband and two boys come to know Jesus Christ as their personal Savior.

"As you look back on your life," I asked Caroline one day, "what do you think triggered your agoraphobia?"

"My mother had a severe case," she replied. "I remember going shopping with her one day. As we were walking next to a wall, her breathing became heavy, and she collapsed. I thought my mother was going to die. I was able to get her home to bed. She had me call the Christian Science practitioner. She came and talked to her and calmed her down for the time being. My mother became worse, however, and it seemed to have an effect on me. I began to panic every time we went out together. My mother would accept dinner engagements then at the last minute she would freeze.

"Caroline, you have to go in my place," she'd say, "I'm just not up to it."

"I felt so awkward," Caroline said, "I'd always have to make some kind of excuse. I don't know why her friends didn't give up on her.

"My mother developed cancer but denied being ill. 'I'm not sick. I'm made in the image of God and I'm perfect,' she'd say.

"The practitioner had convinced my mother that it was so.

"I stayed and took care of my mother until she died. I had a lot of bitterness and resentment for a long time. But now I'm free. The Lord has delivered me from that burden too.

"I was also able to resolve a long-standing conflict I had with my cousin. She had hurt me badly. I was angry and wrote her a scathing letter. My mother died last year, and as I thought about life, I realized that at its best it's short. There isn't time for quarrels and bad feelings. I wrote another letter telling my cousin I was sorry for my part and that I loved her.

"Just today she and her husband stopped over to pick up her mother who had spent a few days with me. It was the first time I had seen her in a very long time. I greeted her at the door with a hug. Once again I told her I loved her. When she left, I hugged her again and told her I loved her. Her only response was, 'Well, I'm not dead yet.'

"It really doesn't matter to me what other people's responses are," she said, "I just want to be sure my heart's attitude is right before the Lord. It was a relief to be able to tell someone I loved them and not worry about the response."

We who have been raised in Christian homes have a lot to be thankful for. How easy it is to take for granted the goodness of the Lord.

9

What Would You Have Said—

When the Clerk Started to Wait on You, and You Realized It Wasn't Your Turn?

I patiently waited my turn to order the Danish pastry I had been eyeing at the bakery. I didn't see anyone ahead of me so I said to the clerk, "I have number thirteen."

"I don't know what happened to number twelve," the clerk said, as he looked around. "I don't see anyone else, so I guess you're next, lady," He took my number.

As I was giving him my order, a man walked up and said, "Wait a minute! My number is twelve."

"I'd better wait on him first," the clerk said apologetically.

"I'm terribly sorry," I said, "I didn't mean to get ahead of you. It was my fault."

"No, it was my fault," the man insisted. "I was standing here talking to my friend. I really wasn't paying attention."

"It was my fault," his friend added. "I shouldn't have been talking to him."

Then with a smile and half-laughing, the clerk said, "Actually it was my fault. I didn't call his number!"

By that time we all had a good laugh, and no one was offended.

"I think it's great that all of us were willing to take the blame," I said. "That's rather unusual these days. Most people would say, 'It's not my fault' or 'you're to blame.' When it comes right down to it, all of us are guilty.

"It's just like God's requirement to get to heaven," I continued.

"Yeah, what's that?" one of the men asked.

"We have to admit we're sinners, that we're wrong, and can't measure up to God's perfect standard," I replied.

"Tell it to him again," his friend said. "That's exactly what I told him last Sunday. He's got to confess he's a sinner." They looked at me to verify it.

"That's absolutely correct," I answered. "You have to confess to God that you're a sinner."

"Okay, I confess. Now what?"

"You've gotten a good start, but you have to receive Jesus Christ as your Savior. He's the only one who can save you from your sin."

The man seemed interested, and it appeared that he wanted to talk further, but his friend said, "Take your baked goods, and we'll talk about it on the way home. Thanks for setting my friend straight," he said to me good-naturedly.

The clerk smiled and said, "That was an interesting conversation."

"We've had a lot of fun but what was said was gospel truth," I said.

"It will give me something to think about," the clerk replied.

Number 14 was waiting to give her order. I took my package and left.

I was conscious of the fact that even in fun, we can say a word for the Lord.

I have also discovered I can witness when people are fearful about things they can't control—like the woman I met at the grocery store.

"What do you think about the strange weather we've been experiencing lately?"

I turned to see to whom the woman was speaking. My back was turned to her, so it surprised me when I realized she was speaking to me.

"You mean the drought we had last summer and now the rains?" I asked.

"Yes—and also the hurricanes. What do you make of it?"

This stranger actually expected me to give my opinion, so I said, "I think God is trying to get our attention."

"What do you mean?" she asked.

"Have you noticed that when things go well in our lives, we don't pay much attention to God? But when we're in trouble, the first thing we say is 'Lord, help me.' Then if he doesn't come to our rescue we become angry with God and blame him for our problems."

"You're probably right, I haven't thought about it that way before."

"According to the Bible," I went on, "God created us to have fellowship with him. He really loves us. He doesn't want us to use him like a Santa Claus. He wants us to be his friends. Sometimes he has to hit us over the head to get our attention."

"You've given me a lot of food for thought, and you just might be right."

I then had to give my attention to the cashier as she checked out my groceries.

There is never much time to talk at the checkout counter, but I had a chance to answer a question that troubled a customer. Perhaps the seed will be germinated by someone else. I don't always have the opportunity to share the gospel when involved in conversation, but God can use the little that is said. We can trust him with the rest.

I pray that this woman will think about what was said and that she will have other questions about God.

I rarely go shopping or leave the house for any reason that I don't find an opportunity to say something for the Lord. I don't plan to do this. It just comes up in the course of things.

Last week, while trying on a sweater, I met a woman. We were comparing our finds and commenting on them. I noticed that she was wearing a cross. It was about an inch and a half long. She also had on some gold chains. After commenting on our purchases, I said, "That's a beautiful cross you're wearing. Tell me, what does it mean to you?"

"It means I'm Presbyterian."

"Oh. What I mean is, what does the cross mean to you personally?"

"It means I follow Jesus when it comes to the Golden Rule."

"I had hoped you would say it represents the fact that Jesus Christ died on the cross for your sins, and that you have accepted him as your personal Savior."

"No, I don't believe that. I just believe in his teaching. You know—the Golden Rule."

I smiled and said, "I love reading the Bible daily. It has so much more to it than the Golden Rule. It has the answer to life—eternal life."

That's all I could say. I hope it caused her to think. I prayed that night that God would give her a hunger to know his Word and find eternal life in his Son.

Looking Back

As I reflect back on these experiences, I am aware that much sowing and watering of the seed has to be done before there can be any reaping. Whatever God has called us to do on a particular day, he requires faithfulness. It is so exciting to think God would allow us to have a part in bringing someone to himself.

In the case of the man at the bakery, I learned that God can use a bit of humor to get a truth across. In fact I've found that a little light-heartedness goes a long way. It can often be turned into a serious discussion. It appeared that the two men were planning just that as they traveled home from the bakery.

As I was driving home, I was reminded of Jesus who could find an illustration in the ordinary things of life. He said, "I am the bread of life. He who comes to me will never go hungry, and he who believes in me will never be thirsty" (John 6:35).

Every time we buy or eat bread, we are reminded of the "Bread of Life," Jesus Christ. When we turn on the light in a dark room, we are reminded of the Light of the World. How awful it would be to live in complete darkness! When we go swimming or boating, we are reminded that as human beings we can't walk on water or command the storm to be still. But Jesus did. These illustrations can be openers to talk to someone about the Lord.

We can take the little we have and know and share it with people who are confused about the events happening in this world. We then trust God to use it.

In the case of the woman with the gold cross, I have many fine Presbyterian friends who have accepted Jesus Christ as their personal Savior. Just because a person says she belongs to a certain denomination is no guarantee that she is a believer. We shouldn't automatically take for granted that she has accepted Jesus Christ as her personal Savior. We just can't lump people together. Salvation is a personal matter, not a group event.

10

What Would You Have Said—

When the Room Your Group Had Reserved Was Given to Another Party, and They Gave You the Lounge Instead?

The bartender, a young woman in her early twenties, listened attentively as I gave my testimony. She put her elbows on the counter and with her head in her hands, she seemed to concentrate on what I was saying.

What was I, a committed Christian, speaking to other committed believers, doing in a place that served drinks? Let me tell you the rest of the story.

My husband was asked to drive a busload of "Seasoned Saints" from our church, many of whom were role models to me as I grew up. They had faithfully served the Lord as Sunday school teachers, youth sponsors, and church board and committee members.

John Orme, our associate pastor, asked me to come along and give a brief message. "I will be delighted," I said. I never dreamed I'd ever be able to minister to these special friends, many of whom had lost their mates and needed Christian fellowship. *What a privilege* I thought.

We arrived at a quaint little inn overlooking the St. Claire River at exactly noon. Pastor Orme had made arrangements previously for us to use one of the small, private dining rooms. "Stay here on the bus until I double-check on the location of our room," he said.

He looked disappointed when he returned. "I'm sorry. They have switched rooms. We will have to use the lounge. They did promise, however, not to serve drinks while we are there." He explained this to the satisfaction of the seniors. (Later, contrary to that promise, a few people were allowed in and were quietly served alcohol, but they were not intrusive and left quickly).

It was not at all what we had planned, but most of us focused our attention on the beautiful view of the river rather than on the inconvenience.

Remember the bartender? She stayed there, quietly observing us. No one else seemed to pay any attention to her but she intrigued me. She was very attractive, and I appreciated her poise and lack of resentment at our being there. She knew we wouldn't be ordering drinks from the bar!

I sat in a corner, sizing up the situation and wondering how I would handle it, when my friend Ruth Long, who was sitting at the next table, whispered loudly, "Nellie, how are you going to handle this one? Maybe you should change your message," she said with a twinkle in her eye.

"I've been sitting here seriously thinking about that."

Then I thought, *This room was given to us. I'm the speaker so why not take advantage of the situation?*

I began to pray, "Lord, I'm prepared to speak to the senior citizens today but the bartender has needs too. Please give me a message for both."

After our dessert, the pastor introduced me as their speaker. I noticed the bartender was listening.

As I walked to the middle of the room, I didn't know exactly what I was going to say, but I *did* know God was in control.

Where I stood, I was separated from my audience by a railing and was unable to see the young woman leaning on the bar behind me.

"As I look around the room," I said, "I want to thank all of you who have been an encouragement to me. Your influence has helped make me the kind of person I am today."

What do I say now? Give your testimony. The thought flashed through my mind.

What I said next was not planned. I began, "Many of you may not know that as a young teenager I sometimes skipped church and spent my collection money at the corner drugstore. I didn't do it all the time, just once in a while, when I thought I wouldn't get caught. Oh, I read the Bible and even memorized Scripture verses but reading the Bible in those days was like reading my history book. I believed it, but it didn't affect my life.

"One day when I began to listen, not only with my head but with my heart, I began to realize the great sacrifice Jesus Christ made for me when he died on the cross for my sins. By dying in my place, he chose to be my substitute. He who knew no sin became sin for me. I was overwhelmed. I didn't deserve it, and I couldn't work for it. All I could do was to accept what Jesus Christ did for me on the cross as a gift. I received him as my Savior. He took all my guilt on himself, and I went scot-free. And because of his forgiveness, I have peace. And to think, when I die I will go to heaven and be with him. That is tremendous security.

"After years of sharing my experience, I have seen God work in other lives besides my own.

"I gave a series of Bible studies at a Lutheran church a few years ago. We were studying the Book of Galatians. I noticed a woman sitting in the audience, arms folded, and looking at me as though to say, 'Now what do you think you can teach me?' It made me feel a bit uneasy but I went on to explain as Paul was addressing the people in Galatia, he said, 'Grace and peace to you . . . ' [1:3].

"You can't have God's peace in your life until you've experienced his grace.

"At the close of the session the woman with the folded arms came up to me and said, 'I guess I don't have God's grace because I certainly don't have his peace. Could you help me?'

"I explained to the woman that until we confess we are sinners before a holy God and accept Jesus Christ as our Savior, we will not have peace.

"'Oh, I know I'm a sinner and I would love to be forgiven and experience his peace.'

"Yes, she accepted Jesus Christ as her Savior.

"I had mistaken her folded arms and the stern expression on her face as belligerence. Later she told me, 'I was desperate for help.' It is so easy to judge people by outward appearances, isn't it?"

The senior citizens were delighted to hear about what God had been doing in my life. They were glad the message was shared with the young woman at the bar. Perhaps that's why they clapped when I finished speaking.

As we prepared to leave several of the seniors came to me and said, "I'm so glad you shared your testimony with us today. The bartender was listening so earnestly."

I decided to go back into the lounge after the group left. I walked up to the young woman serving at the bar and said, "We had a lovely time today. The view of the river is so beautiful. It has been a very pleasant day for the seniors." Then I noticed she was wearing a cross. "Your cross is beautiful. What does it mean to you?"

She smiled and hesitatingly said, It—umm . . . well, it means . . . a lot."

I was conscious of all my friends waiting for me on the bus, so I briefly stated what the cross meant to me. "When I see a cross, I am reminded that Jesus Christ died for me: that he took on himself the guilt and penalty of my sin. I've accepted Christ as my Savior and now I have peace. I don't have to worry about the future. It's all in God's hands.

"I would like to give you a booklet. It explains the basics of the Bible. Would you like to take it home and read it? Then see if it makes sense to you?"

"Is it Christian?" she asked.

"Oh, yes."

"Then I'll take it. You see I am getting married in two weeks. My fiance and I have been going to the priest for instructions."

"If you want a good marriage, I suggest that you and your new husband read a portion of the Bible together each day. My husband and I do that. If you obey what the Bible says, I'll guarantee you'll have a good marriage."

"Oh, thank you," she said. "We do so much want to have a good marriage. I get frightened when I hear about so many divorces. I'm really going to work on my marriage."

Looking Back

We don't always know the situations where we will be placed. We do know that God is sovereign and never makes a mistake. None of us would choose to have our lunch in a lounge, but there was no other choice. Yes, the inn had let us down, but Pastor Orme graciously accepted the inconvenience. That in turn put the senior citizens at ease.

I am reminded that Jesus ate with the publicans and sinners. He showed them love.

We, too, as a body of believers must follow Jesus' example and show love to those who are without.

We teased Pastor Orme later and told him. "You really didn't need to apologize for the room we were given. It gave us an opportunity to share the gospel with a stranger, a most unlikely person—a beautiful bartender."

11

What Would You Have Said—

When Your New Jewish Friend Said, "I Have One God and You Have Three. Please Explain"?

Sarah

I was driving down a well-traveled road in our area when my attention was drawn to an object in the middle of the street. My curiosity caused me to stop the car.

I parked at the side of the road and picked up what looked like a textbook. Then I discovered it was a Jewish prayerbook. Written on the fly leaf was printed: PRESENTED TO SARAH ROTH FROM RABBI ABRAHAM 1967. There was no address in the book.

When I got home, I called the nearby Jewish temple and told them my story. "Is Rabbi Abraham still at your temple?" I asked. And do you have a Sarah Roth on your records?"

"The rabbi is no longer with us," she said. "Let me look in the files to see if the young woman's name is listed."

When the secretary returned she said, "I'm sorry, we have no such name on our records. "I suggest you bring the prayerbook to us."

"What will you do with the book?" I asked.

"We will put it in the Lost and Found."

"I don't think that's such a good idea. After all, if she isn't a member of your synagogue, she won't be looking for her book there," I answered.

"It belongs here. You should really bring it to us."

"I will first try to find the rightful owner. If I can't find her, then I'll bring it to you."

I prayed: "Heavenly Father, I don't believe it was an accident that I found the Jewish prayerbook. Please help me to find the rightful owner. Show me how I can be of help."

I looked in the phone book to see if I could find her name.

There were twenty-five people by that name in the directory. *The only thing to do is to start calling,* I thought.

"I am looking for a Sarah Roth. Am I calling the right number?" I asked.

"No, there is no one by that name living here."

"Do you know anyone by that name?" I questioned.

I was getting a bit discouraged but decided I would call all twenty-five names if I had to.

Finally, by the tenth phone call, the woman answering said, "Sarah is my daughter. Her name is no longer Roth since she is now married. Her name is Rosenthal now. She is not at home. May I give her a message?"

"I found a prayerbook in the middle of Thirteen Mile Road with your daughter's name in it."

"Oh, thank you," she said. "You have no idea how badly my daughter felt when she realized she had lost it. The prayerbook never meant so much to her until she couldn't find it."

"If you give me your address, I'll bring it to her," I said.

"Sarah is taking flying lessons right now. I'll call the airport and leave a message. She will be ever so grateful. I'm sure she'll want to meet you. I'll tell her to stop by your house on the way home. It will probably be around three-thirty."

I was sitting in the family room preparing the lesson for my Bible-study class when she arrived.

I invited the young woman to come in. She was tall and slim, probably in her thirties. She had a gracious charm about her that was immediately noticeable.

"I can't tell you how much I appreciate your finding my prayerbook," she said. "It is something I treasure. We were on the way to the temple to celebrate Yom Kippur when I lost it. My hands were full, so I put the book on the roof of my car and forgot about it. When I got to the temple I remembered but, of course, it was gone."

"I'm glad I was able to locate you," I said. "I lost my Bible once. I was in a hurry to go shopping, and it must have fallen out of the car as I opened the door to get out. A Jewish family found it and called my church. I had left a bulletin in it with the address of my church.

"I thought of that incident when I found your prayerbook. I asked God to help me find you. He answered my prayer.

"That was thoughtful," she said.

"It's interesting that you should arrive just now. I was preparing my lesson for our next Bible-study class," I said. "I was reading a verse in the New Testament. It says in Mark 12:10 that the stone the builders rejected, this became the chief cornerstone. It's the same in the Old Testament. See, the exact words are in Psalm 118:22."

Before I could say another word Sarah said, "I know who it is speaking about. Jesus Christ, right? He's the head of your faith."

I couldn't help wonder. *If I had asked my Bible class before they had studied the lesson, would they have known to whom the cornerstone referred?*

I commented on her insight.

"My father once told me I had great understanding about spiritual things and he encouraged me to be open-minded."

"That's incredible," I said. "That means you and I can discuss the Bible without feeling intimidated. We can agree or disagree with each other without getting angry, right?"

"Absolutely," was her response. "I would like to repay you for finding my book and taking the trouble to call me."

"I couldn't possibly accept anything," I said. "I am so happy I found you and now I have met a very special person. I don't want a reward."

"Would you let me take you out to lunch?" she asked. "I have a lot of questions I would like to ask you about your faith."

"I would like that very much. I would like to get to know you better, too," I answered.

She picked me up the following Thursday, and we went to a nearby health-food restaurant.

"No wonder you look so great," I teased. "Eating this kind of food would keep anyone in shape."

She laughed.

"Tell me something about yourself," I said. "Do you have children?"

"Yes, I have two boys and a girl. I'm a practicing attorney, a writer, and I also enjoy flying."

"My, you have quite a full life," I responded.

"I also do some volunteer work. I read to the fourth graders once a week. I enjoy that too."

After we ordered our lunch, Sarah started to ask questions pertaining to my faith. Her questions were legitimate, and I could well understand why she was puzzled about such things as the Trinity.

"Nellie, can you explain why you have three Gods and we only have one?"

"We don't have three Gods. We have one God, but three manifestations of God: the Father, the Son and the Holy Spirit. They are one, and yet they each have a special function," I said.

"The Trinity is a mystery. It can't be explained but we know it is so. The Bible speaks of each one being fully God.

"The Bible also says that Jesus is God in the flesh. Jesus came to show us what the Father is like. We can know God through Jesus Christ.

"Perhaps I can explain it somewhat in human terms. We have water, ice, and steam. They each have three different functions and yet they are one. Also an egg has three parts, the shell, the white, and the yolk, and yet an egg is one and closely related.

"When I asked Jesus Christ to come into my life, it wasn't a man that came to dwell within me it was . . ." before I could finish she said, "It was the Holy Spirit. Am I right?"

Once again I was amazed at her ability to understand. She was polite and listened as I shared with her my belief that Jesus Christ was the promised Messiah.

Our form of Judaism doesn't believe that Messiah is a person," she explained, "but a final state of being. You might say an age of utopia."

As we drove home, we discussed the Bible.

"If we want to know God, who he is, and what he's like we need to read and study the Scriptures," I said.

"I don't agree with that at all. I don't think we need to read the Bible to know God."

We had agreed not to argue but to explore each others' beliefs, so we let that statement go for a while.

"Do you believe in the Signs of the Zodiac?" she asked.

"No, I don't. It is one of the things God speaks against.

You'll find that in the Old Testament, the eighteenth chapter of Deuteronomy to be exact."

"Well, don't you want to know what my sister told me?"

"What did your sister tell you?" I asked.

"She told me that my spiritual understanding may not necessarily come from my family but from someone else. Maybe you are the one to help me."

"I don't know anything about your family," I said, "but I will be happy to share my knowledge of the Scriptures anytime."

As we continued driving, Sarah said, "I do enjoy reading to the fourth graders. Right now I'm reading them a story by a Russian author. I told the teacher that I would like to take some time to tell them about the man who wrote the story. It would give them an understanding of the background of the story. The teacher doesn't want me to take the time. She doesn't feel it is necessary to tell them about the author. I totally disagree."

Sarah seemed a little put out. I was glad to see her a little fired up about it.

"What do you think?" she asked. "Do you agree that I should tell the children about the author? Don't you think that would help them understand the story better?" she asked.

"Absolutely," I answered. "That's exactly what I mean about getting to know God. The only way we can get to know him is by reading his Word, the Bible."

"I get the point," she said. "Tell me which Bible to get, and where do I start reading?"

What a delightful person, I thought. It was refreshing to see a person with her abilities not puffed up with pride. She was actually open to learn.

"Would you like to visit our church to see what it's like?" I asked.

"I would love to," she answered.

The following Sunday, she came to our home. The three

of us, Sarah, my husband, and I went to church together. This was a new experience for her. She took it all in.

"I had such a warm feeling while sitting in church," she said. "When the speaker was giving the sermon, I felt like I was sitting by a cozy fire listening to a story. I just loved it."

After the service, I introduced her to many of my friends. She had a hard time understanding why my friend Elise, who is a completed Jew, (one who has recognized Jesus Christ as the Messiah) would become a member of our church. Sarah was very open about it.

"Why would you leave the synagogue?" she asked. "That really puzzles me."

My friend Elise said, "I have to be honest with you. It was too secular. It didn't meet my need. My experience was like that of Paul in the Bible. It was as though I was blind then my eyes were opened and I could see. It has changed my entire life."

Each time Sarah and I met for lunch, we discussed the Bible. I loved being with her.

The next time Sarah came to church with us, she turned to me during the singing of the hymn "He Lives" and said, "I won't be able to sing this song. You understand don't you?"

"Of course I understand. I don't expect you to sing songs about Jesus and I really wouldn't want you to. Only people who have received Christ as Savior and believe in him should sing that song. You can listen and observe. You'll understand better what makes me tick."

I appreciated her honesty.

A few weeks later, Sarah called and said, "My children keep asking me what God is like. Can you help me with that?"

"I believe I can. God has many names. Each one denotes his character, which will help your children know in a small way what God is like. For instance, Moses asked God at his experience with the burning bush, 'Suppose I go back to the Israelites and say to them, "The God of your fathers has sent me to you," and they ask me, "What is his name? "Then what shall I tell them?' God told Moses to tell the Israelites: 'I AM has sent me . . . the God of Abraham, the God of Isaac and the God of Jacob . . .' (Exod. 3:13–15).

"Remember when God asked Abraham to sacrifice his son? God provided a ram in place of Isaac. It was a test and Abraham passed.

"You see, sacrificing their firstborn was a pagan custom. Their offering was to false gods. Would Abraham be willing to do anything less for the true and living God? Was God first in Abraham's life?

"Abraham had faith that his God would provide. He believed the promise God had made to him that he would have a son and his descendents would be like the stars in the sky (Gen. 15).

"God was called Jehovah-Jirah, meaning God will provide.

"God has many names. It is a very interesting study. I'll type up a list of names and references. You'll enjoy going over them with your children."

"I'd really appreciate that!" Sarah seemed excited.

"If I'm not loading you down too much and you're interested, I'd like to give you a list of events that were prophesied in the Old Testament and fulfilled in the New Testament. They were predicted hundreds of years before they came to pass."

"That sounds interesting. I'd like to see your material."

"Did you know that Jesus' birth, death, and resurrection was talked about in the Psalms and in Isaiah? You might want to check it out."

One day, Sarah called. She was very excited. "I have something interesting to tell you. I was doing some volunteer work for the opera, and one of the women in the group started to tell me some things about the Bible. I was interested but told her I'd have to check it out with my Bible teacher."

"What is your teacher's name?" the woman asked.

"I told her that my teacher's name is Nellie Pickard."

"I know her. She's a friend of mine," the woman answered.

"I was so excited," Sarah said, "I just had to call you and tell you about it."

We continued to have lunch from time to time. Each time we discussed biblical truths. We had a wonderful time together.

As time went on Sarah's workload became heavier. Her family needed her, and she wanted to continue flying so there wasn't much time for us to get together.

We, in the meantime, moved into a townhouse and began to spend five or six months in Florida.

My speaking schedule was heavy and I worked hard on my book *What Do You Say When . . .* There seemed to be many demands on our time.

Before we left for Florida that winter, I called her and told her I had written a book.

"We are on our way to church right now. May I stop by and give you a copy? I know you may not agree with my writing but I'd like your opinion anyway."

"I'm so proud of you, Nellie," she said. "I would love a copy of your book."

We dropped it off and continued on to the evening service.

I really didn't know how she would receive the stories of one person after another receiving Christ. It was important for me to know.

I didn't hear from her while we were in Florida. When we got home in April, I called her and asked if she would be available for lunch.

"We can discuss my book. I'm eager to know what you think about it," I said. We had lunch the following week.

Sarah had been in court that morning so I waited in her office for her to arrive.

I was a bit tense as I tried to concentrate on a magazine article I was reading. *I hope I didn't make a mistake by letting her read my book,* I thought. *Maybe she'll think I was presumptuous by giving it to her, knowing she didn't believe in Jesus Christ.*

As these thoughts were going through my mind, Sarah walked in.

We looked at each other, and then Sarah opened her arms and we both hugged.

"Nellie, I loved your book," were her first words.

I was greatly relieved.

During lunch we discussed my book.

"Nellie, you and I are more alike than you realize," she said. "You try to help people find God, and you are doing a good work. I too, try to help people. I work with abused children and alcoholic parents. It's so sad to see these hurting children. I try to do everything possible to help them. I really work hard for them.

"I can relate to so many things you say in your book. Remember when you told how you and your husband had agreed that you wouldn't spend more than $25.00 on any item without consulting each other? You said money was tight in those early years. Then you said that you saw something you really wanted and it was beyond the agreed amount. You bought it anyway. Then you felt badly."

"Yes, I remember."

"You confessed that to Jesus. Now I would do the same thing. But I would confess it to God."

Yes, Sarah and I are alike in many ways. The big difference is, Jesus Christ is Lord of my life. God the Father sent his Son to die on the cross for my sins and the Spirit of God lives in me, teaching me, convicting, convincing, and guiding me in all truth. He also is my comforter.

On the way out of the restaurant Sarah said, "Nellie, I love Jesus. I think he is a wonderful person."

Of course I wish she knew him as her Savior but that is something beyond my control. Only the Spirit of God can convince her of that. I will leave her in his hands.

"Don't let it be such a long time before we get together again," she said.

Looking Back

Knowing Sarah has been a delightful experience. I called her the other day and read this chapter to her. I wanted to know if it would offend her if *our* story were published.

"I think it's beautiful. I would love to have it as a chapter in your book."

Sarah is not her real name. That is the name she has taken temporarily so my readers could eavesdrop on our friendship. She is truly a generous person.

We plan to see each other soon. Only God knows our future. It's wise to trust him in all things.

12

What Would You Have Said—

When the Chairperson at the Bible Study Was Reluctant to Do the Class Assignment?

Dorcas

Dorcas was an exceptional leader, full of life and always ready and willing to do anything that would further the cause of Christ. She was the chairperson for our Bible-study group. Everyone seemed to love her, and I enjoyed working with her too.

Perhaps that's the reason I was somewhat puzzled when her usual exuberance about an experiment I had suggested wasn't there. She even seemed reluctant to be a part of it. The rest of the class appeared interested.

"This idea is not original with me," I said. "My friend Carol tried it in one of her classes and felt it was most profitable. You don't have to participate in this project if you don't care to, but I think it will end up being a blessing to all of us.

"This is what you're to do: Write a letter to each of your children, and tell them all the good things you've tucked away in your heart—things you have told your friends because you were so proud of them—things you neglected to tell them for one reason or another. You are not to say anything negative. You mention only the positive. In about two weeks, we'll share the experiences."

The following week one of the women came up to me before class started. With a big smile on her face she said, "I wrote my letters and I feel real good about it. I hope my children do."

The time finally came for the women to share their experiences. Several were eager to tell their story.

One woman said, "I wrote to my daughter in Chicago and told her the qualities in her that I appreciated. A few days later, a letter came back in return. As I opened the envelope and unfolded the paper, it had one word written on it: 'Wow.' I understood what it meant. I think it was a giant step of growth in our relationship. I'm glad I participated."

Another woman got up and said, "I haven't spoken to my father for eight years. I wrote him a letter asking his forgiveness for my attitude. He immediately called me and, he not only forgave me but confessed he hadn't been the father he should have been. I plan to see him soon," she said, as she choked down the tears.

To clear the air I told them that I too had written to my children. I told them about the letter I had written to my son and the strange response I had received. He was in law school at the time. I told him how pleased I was with him, for the choices he had made in life, for the hard worker he was, and the lovely girl he had married. My greatest joy, I told him, was that he trusted Christ as his Savior.

My son's response was unexpected. He called on the

phone one day, and without announcing who he was said, "When's the next one coming?"

"The next *what?*" I asked.

"The next letter telling me all my faults."

"There is no next letter." We were both laughing as I hung up.

I told the class that I, too, was glad I had written to my children—that it was long overdue.

According to the results thus far, I think this has been a worthwhile project.

Would anyone else like to share their experience?" I asked.

Dorcas hesitated at first, then she said, "To be truthful, I really did not want to take part in this assignment, but since I'm the chairperson of this group I felt it wouldn't look right if I didn't cooperate. You see, it was easy to write to two of my boys. The youngest hadn't yet reached the rebellious stage and the oldest had seen the error of his ways. He had settled down nicely. But Steve—he was right in the middle of teenage rebellion. He's been such a problem lately. As I sat down to write, I thought, *What can I say to him?* I couldn't think of a thing. I began to cry; then I began to pray. 'Lord, isn't there one good thing about Steve?' Then I remembered, Steve was a great help to me when Gramma came to live with us. She wasn't too easy to get along with but Steve had a way with her, and she loved him. *I could tell him how much I appreciated that,* I thought. Then something else came to my mind. *He really does keep his room neat, and that means a lot to me.* Before I knew it many other things came to my mind that I appreciated about him. Then I thanked the Lord for bringing these things to my attention.

She told us that she was tempted to tell him a few of his faults but remembered that was not allowed in this assignment.

"I finished the letter and put it on his pillow, and the

next day I found a note on my pillow. It said, 'I don't know what what to say, Mom, but thanks.'"

That act of love changed their relationship.

Steve went off to college. Three months later he called his mom. "I'd like to come home next week and bring a friend. I want him to see how our family loves each other." That weekend Steve led his friend to Christ.

I was so pleased at the results of this experiment that I tried it again. I had been invited to hold a series of Bible studies at a church on the east side of our city. It was supposed to be a women's group but several men attended. They were deacons checking me out. You see it was a different denomination from mine. Of course they had to check out my theology. They discovered everything was fine, and some asked if they could continue to attend. They even did their weekly assignments.

One deacon said, "I must confess, I have been pretty hard on my son. He's a doctor and makes hospital rounds every Sunday morning. I have been getting after him for not attending church. I shouldn't have been so hard on him. It really didn't do any good because he didn't pay any attention to me. I decided I would write him a letter just as you asked. You see it finally dawned on me that on Sunday mornings he was ministering to people. He was doing God's work. I told him, 'I'm proud of you son. I've been so wrong in nagging you about church attendance. Will you forgive me?'"

Not only did he forgive his dad but rearranged his schedule so that he was able to attend church services with his family.

One of the sweetest stories that came out of this experiment was when one of the mothers sent her five-year-old son a letter. She told him how special he was and that she loved him very much. He didn't know how to read, so he asked his sister to read the letter to him.

When he got ready for bed that night, he sidled up to his

mom and said, "Could that little boy you love so much have a cookie before he goes to bed?"

"Of course I gave him a cookie. This was an exception, wasn't it?"

Looking Back

It's amazing isn't it? When we do what's right and ask God by his Spirit to lead us, the results are unbelievable. It ought to teach us a lesson.

How easy it is to get irritated at the disagreeable incidents in life, whether they are caused by things or people. We try to work these out in our own way and fail.

If only we could learn to commit our ways "unto the Lord." Most of us have to learn the hard way. Eight years is a long time to be silent with a loved one. Dorcas cried and struggled and then called on the Lord. He is always there when we call on him. He says so in Psalm 50:15:

> and call upon me in the day of trouble;
> I will deliver you and you will honor me.

Dorcas did just that and was rewarded.

My own son discovered that I was really proud of him.

The doctor was not a child to be ordered around but he responded to love.

The little five-year-old boy responded to love. It must have been easier to obey his mom after that.

Christians are to be known by their love. Learning a truth brings the greatest blessing when we act on it.

13

What Would You Have Said—

When You Stepped Out of Line for a Moment and Found Someone Had Taken Your Place?

I stepped out of line just for a moment. I wanted to check the price of the two-pound box of chocolates at the next counter. The price was horrendous. As I started to get back in line, a woman stepped in front of me.

I said, "Oops, that's what I get for stepping out of line. I shouldn't have looked temptation in the face. Can you believe a two-pound box of candy costs twelve dollars and seventy-five cents? And they call this a *discount* store? Back in the good old days that same box of candy cost five dollars and ninety-five cents!"

We both laughed and shook our heads in disbelief. Then the woman said, "Come on, get in line. You didn't lose your place. I saved it for you."

How kind, I thought.

The woman looked at my purchases. *"Fisherman's Friend. I'm curious. What is that?"*

"They are throat lozenges. I bought them for my pastor. That is, he used to be my pastor but now he's the president of Moody Bible Institute. When we met him in Florida last month, he had to speak four times in one day. And, believe me, it took a toll on his throat.

"I had some of these lozenges with me and gave him some. It helped him immediately. I promised I would get some for him as soon as I got back to Michigan. This store is the only place I know of that carries them."

"They're really good, huh? Have you tried them yourself?" she asked.

"I do quite a bit of speaking and use them all the time. It keeps me from coughing."

"Tell me what do you speak about?" (I had hoped she'd ask.)

"I tell people about Jesus Christ, and how they can have their sins forgiven. I tell them what the Bible says and God's requirements to be in his family."

"That's the most exciting thing I've heard in a long time," she said. "I know about Moody Bible Institute. We used to live in Chicago. My son just recently went to some function there.

"Let me show you something," she said as she opened her purse, took out a notebook, turned the pages until she came to the one she was looking for. "Look at this," she smiled.

I read: Romans 3:23; Romans 6:23; Romans 5:8; John 1:12, and several other Bible verses.

With her face aglow, she said, "I'm memorizing these verses so I can be better prepared to witness.

"To think this all happened because I let you get in front of me. Isn't the Lord good?" she said.

God gives us so many goodies along the way when we take the opportunities that come before us. It makes life exciting and gives us a real purpose for living. My friend Virginia had been conversing with the woman in front of her at the grocery store. They both spotted the tabloids on the shelf next to the cash register. My friend said, "Those papers are just a bunch of lies. I don't believe a word they say."

"You're probably right, but what is truth anyway?" the woman asked.

"Why, Jesus Christ is truth. He said, 'I am the way, the truth and the life. No one comes to the Father but by me.'"

The woman didn't say a word. She turned and finished her business and went on her way.

I was proud of Virginia. She knew what truth was and wasn't afraid to speak up. The answer may have fallen on deaf ears or—perhaps it gave the woman something to think about.

I walked over to the office center with my husband to pick up the *Wall Street Journal* one morning. As we were walking down the hall, I overheard two women behind me talking rather loudly. They were probably secretaries. One of the girls kept saying, "Oh, my God."

After repeating this three or four times, I just had to turn around and say something.

"Did you say, 'Oh, my God?'" I asked. She looked puzzled and then said, "Yeah."

As kindly as possible I said, "God is holy. His name should not be taken in vain. It hurts me to hear you use his name in that manner."

Immediately her friend spoke up. She seemed relieved that I had addressed the issue. "I know what you're talking about. I'm Catholic, and my sister is a nun. I know we shouldn't take God's name in vain."

"Because I'm a believer in Jesus Christ," I said, "I want to honor his name."

"I'm Jewish," the offender said.

"Then you really should know God's laws, right?"

"I suppose so, but I don't."

She smiled and walked away.

Looking Back

What would you have said if someone asked you if you had ever used the lozenges you were buying? In my pre-witnessing days, I probably would have said, "Yes, I've tried them and they work."

Now I took it as an opportunity. I threw out my bait. I told her I found them helpful when I had to speak. She nibbled at the bait.

"What do you speak about?" she asked.

That question opened up a conversation that ended in blessing for both of us.

In the case of Virginia, what would you have said? Would you have had courage to quote a Scripture verse if someone asked you, "What is truth?"

Spiritually it puts us on the spot. We have to make instant decisions as to whether we will take the opportunity standing before us, begging to be taken.

What about the girl who took God's name in vain?

I don't know why I felt compelled to speak up that day. Perhaps it was because the young woman was defaming the name of my best friend. It always cuts me to the core when I hear someone take God's name in vain. I spoke the truth in love. I pray that our conversation will stay in her memory and cause her to think about God, his holiness, power, and beauty.

Second Timothy 4:2–5 says:

Preach the Word; be prepared in season and out of season; correct, rebuke and encourage—with great patience and careful instruction. For the time will come when men will not put up with sound doctrine. Instead, to suit their own desires, they will gather around them a great number of teachers to say what their itching ears want to hear. They will turn their ears away from the truth and will turn aside to myths. But you keep your head in all situations, endure hardship, do the work of an evangelist, discharge all the duties of an evangelist.

Paul wrote this to Timothy. We can learn from these verses that we should take every opportunity to speak up for our Lord. Let people know that we are on his side.

14

What Would You Have Said—

When Your Friend in the Nursing Home Didn't Recognize You?

"R. E., can you tell this nurse how she can be sure she will go to heaven when she dies?"

Robert Ernest Thompson, better known as R. E., had served the Lord in China for many years. He then established Missionary Internship, an organization which trains young men and women for the mission field. We often called him "Our Missionary Statesman."

I sat under the Rev. Thompson's ministry many times. He preached the gospel clearly and with fervor. I had often said to him, "R. E., you have been such a blessing in my life. You've taught me many things about the Christian life. I want to thank you."

"Well, now, you'd better be careful or I'll get a swelled head," he'd say in his beautiful Irish brogue. But now there was a problem. He was suffering from Alzheimer's disease and had to be taken to a nursing home. It was sad to see him in that condition. Even though he had been in our home many times, he now did not recognize me.

Now his body had been afflicted with this dread disease which affects the memory long before the patients are physically disabled.

One day, while visiting the nursing home, I asked him, "Can you explain to this nurse what it means to be 'born again'?"

I knew he was familiar with this term. I'd heard him use it often.

He turned to me and in a very clear precise voice said, "Now the first thing you have to do is to confess to God that you're a sinner. Then you need to receive Jesus Christ as your personal Savior. You can't save yourself, you know."

"Is that all you do?" I asked.

"No," he hesitated a moment and went on, "then after you've done that, tell him you want to be his child, and want to live for him. That's about it."

His nurse was amazed, and so was I. It was proof that though his flesh and his mind were weak, the Spirit was strong. I left that nursing home uplifted. A sick man with Alzheimer's disease had ministered to me that day.

My husband's parents were in the same nursing home. My father-in-law had had a stroke. It affected his speech so he couldn't talk. We would sometimes sing hymns when we visited him. He sang right along with us as clearly as though he hadn't been affected by the stroke. We often read or quoted Scripture. He had memorized great portions of the Bible and would repeat or mouth the words along with us. He always carried a small New Testament with him. He would show it to us from time to time, indicating to us that it was very important to him. We could not carry on a normal conversation with him but his eyes would light up when we talked about his Savior.

It was hard to see this man, who at one time had lived a

very productive life, now needing help in almost everything he did. Once I told his nurse, a perfect stranger to him, "Would you believe that for years my father-in-law was the superintendent of our Sunday school and also chairman of the Christian Business Men's Committee in our area?"

She shook her head and said, "Strange what happens to people, isn't it?"

"Have you ever heard him sing hymns and quote Scripture?"

"Yes, I have and that's an amazement to me," she said.

"He's forgotten most of the things that ever happened to him in life," I said, "but he never forgets Jesus Christ. To me that's remarkable."

My friend Sam was dying of Lou Gehrig's disease (ALS). He too was in that same nursing home. His mind was sharp as it was not affected by his illness. We visited him often and had long talks. But as time went on his speech became more and more slurred. We strained to understand him. He then began to use a pad and pencil in order to communicate with us.

Sam was a completed Jew, a most remarkable man. He had accepted Christ while mowing his lawn one day. His manager, Harry Johnson, at work had shared the Scriptures with him on several occasions. One day it hit him hard. *Jesus Christ is the Messiah. I know he is,* were his thoughts.

When he announced to his family that he had become a believer in Jesus Christ, he was immediately rejected. He was not allowed to eat with the family and had to live in the basement of his home—but he was expected to pay the bills.

I don't know what caused his illness but he could not continue to live in the basement any longer. He moved to Florida but continued to support the family financially.

Sam never complained. He continued to pray for his

family, that they too would come to know Jesus Christ as their Savior. He asked all of his friends to join him. It wasn't easy for him to leave his family as he cared for them deeply.

Even though we knew he was ill, none of his friends suspected he had Lou Gehrig's disease. A year later he was forced to go to a nursing home. He just couldn't take care of himself any longer.

We visited this special man often. We wanted to encourage him.

"Sam," I said, "We'll be going up north shortly but expect to come back in a few months. We'll see you then."

Sam shook his head and pointed his finger upward. With a smile he tried to say, "Heaven, heaven."

I knew what he meant. He knew it wouldn't be long before he would be with his Savior. He was looking forward to that time.

Sam was greatly loved because of his stand for Jesus Christ.

People visited him daily and prayed with him. The nurses commented on his many friends.

One day as I visited him, I noticed his new roommate. I introduced myself and he told me his name was Mr. Peartree. "I'm here on a temporary basis. I have my own apartment and expect to return after they finish with my tests."

"Do you have a family in the area?" I asked.

"No, I'm sorry to say, I don't have a family in the area, so I never have visitors. My wife died a year ago and my son lives in Massachusetts. I'm really all alone."

"Don't you have a church home here?" I asked.

"No, I haven't gone to church for quite a while. I do notice that Sam has lots of visitors from his church. It must be nice. They always pray with him. No one ever prays with me."

"That can be easily remedied," I said. "I visit here quite

often and I promise I will stop and see you and pray with you."

I told him about Sam and how his family had rejected him when he had accepted Jesus Christ as his Savior.

"Being a Jewish Christian isn't always easy," I remarked. "Sam had to make a choice between Jesus Christ and his family. He's looking forward to being with his Savior.

"I wish the two of you could talk more; but even though Sam has a keen mind, his speech is slurred and it is difficult for people to understand him. You can talk to him though, and he will communicate somehow."

Then I said, "Tell me something about yourself. Have you always lived in Florida?"

"No, actually I'm from Atlanta. The mailmen always got a kick out of delivering my mail—my name being Peartree, and I lived on Peachtree Street in Atlanta."

"I bet you've had a lot of fun with your name."

"Yeah, some people think I'm joking when I tell them my name, especially when I tell them the name of my street, but tell me more about Sam."

"Sam is very special," I said. He has taught his friends a lot about loyalty when it comes to his love for the Savior. Jesus Christ means more to him than anything else in the world. He still loves his family and we, along with him, are praying that his wife and children will come to know the Lord, too."

"That's a sad story."

"Yes, in one way, but happy because Sam knows when he dies he will go to heaven and be with God. Tell me, do you believe the Bible when it says that everyone has sinned?"

"Yes, I know that. I've been confessing my sins on a regular basis," he said.

"Have you ever received Jesus Christ as your Savior?" I asked.

"Can't say I've ever done that. Maybe I don't have the complete picture."

"The Bible tells us in the first chapter of John that Jesus Christ was God in the flesh. He came to earth so that we might better understand what God the Father is like. He was without sin and yet he took our sins on himself. Just think, God loved us so much that he was willing to send his only son to die in our place [John 3:16]. If we believe and receive Jesus, we can have everlasting life. Kind of overwhelming isn't it?"

I then shared with him my little booklet that showed him that he too could be in the family of God.

"Look, in Revelation 3:20 Jesus is talking. 'Here I am! I stand at the door and knock. If anyone hears my voice and opens the door, I will come in and eat with him, and he with me.' Jesus is saying that if you will open your heart and invite him into your life, he will be with you and have fellowship with you.

"Mr. Peartree, would you like to receive Jesus Christ as your personal Savior?"

"Yes, I think I'm ready to do that. I've been close many times but I've never taken that step. I would appreciate it very much if you would pray with me."

We bowed our heads and he prayed after me, "Dear Father, I admit that I am a sinner. I believe that the Lord Jesus Christ died for me. I receive him now as my Savior. Thank you for forgiving my sin and for accepting me into your family. In Jesus' name I pray, *Amen.*"

"Mr. Peartree, you are now a brand-new member of the family of God. I want to welcome you into the family."

We shared the good news with Sam, and there was great happiness in that room. Sam's friends stopped to talk and pray with Mr. Peartree, and he was no longer alone. He had a new family, the family of God.

The tests came back shortly after that, and it was discovered that Mr. Peartree had inoperable cancer. He never did have the opportunity to go back to his apartment. Three weeks after his new membership into God's family, God took him home to be with him. He went to a far better home than the apartment he had left.

I have another dear friend I visit in a nursing home in Michigan. Her name is Audie and she is ninety-three years old. Just a few years ago Audie helped with the senior citizens' group at our church. She helped make arrangements for small trips, luncheons, and other interesting adventures. She seemed to have the gift of helps and encouragement. She loved to crochet, and I was the recipient of many beautiful pot holders which she would make as love gifts. To me, she was a very special lady.

The time came when Audie had to be brought to a nursing home. Her memory had failed, and it appeared that life was over for her. At first many of her friends visited her. They would sign her guest book and write some encouraging words alongside their names.

As time went on, she wasn't able to read. She couldn't comprehend or understand what she was reading. I would visit her and she didn't know my name. Most of the time she couldn't remember what happened five minutes previously. For some it didn't seem worth while to even visit her.

"After all she doesn't recognize anyone," some said. "She can't remember from one minute to the next what has been going on. I can't see that it makes any difference to her if we visit her or not."

So the visits have become fewer and fewer. I heard someone say, "I don't understand why God doesn't take her home."

I have reflected on that statement many times. Yes, the Lord could take her home. She's done her work on earth. I believe she was left here for *our* sake. God is keeping her here so we can learn something about ministering to others, about patience and love.

I have been more observant lately. I notice that even though she doesn't know my name, she knows I'm a friend and gives me a big smile, and says, "What brings you here today?"

I love to tell her, "I came to see you, of course. I couldn't think of a better thing to do."

She recognizes love and responds.

Audie has taught me much about human needs. I noticed that Ola, her daughter, put the words of hymns on her bulletin board. They sing every time she visits her. I decided I would do the same. She loves to sing and she knows these hymns by memory.

I visited her recently and decided I'd ask her some questions concerning her faith. I remembered R. E. Thompson's remarkable answers and I am convinced that the Spirit is stronger than the flesh.

"Audie," I asked, "If someone in this place should say to you, 'I would like to go to heaven when I die. How do I get there?' What would you tell them?"

At first she said, "I don't know." Then she gave me a strange look and said, "Well, I'm not sure, except you've *got* to know the Lord."

"Is there anything a person has to confess?" I asked.

"Well, you've got to confess the Lord Jesus."

"Yes, but how about the bad things in us?"

"Oh sure, you have to confess your sin."

Once again I was impressed with the work of the Holy Spirit in a person who doesn't have much physical life left. I prayed with Audie and left. I was walking on air. My friend Audie in the nursing home had ministered to me that day in a way she will never realize.

My heart was moved and warmed as I observed my friend Ola care for her mother. She spoke gently and lovingly as she made sure her sweater was put on properly. I listened as they sang together. It was a beautiful sight. Audie can't keep on tune any more, but she knows the words. They are as much a part of her as breathing.

One day she said to me, "Hymns are all I know. I don't know the other songs."

"You don't need the other songs. You know the best songs," I told her.

"Can you quote any Bible verses?" I asked.

"I'm not sure."

"Let's try John 3:16." I started: 'For God so loved the world . . .' "Audie took over." 'He gave his one and only Son, that whoever believes in him shall not perish but have eternal life.'"

"That is just wonderful," I remarked.

"Well, I guess if he loves us, he'll take care of us," she said.

We quoted a few more verses, sang "Jesus Loves Me," and she remarked, "That's a good song for children isn't it?"

"It certainly is and I think it's good for all of us to know he truly loves us.

On the way out I stopped and talked to the nurse about Audie's singing and quoting Bible verses.

"Oh, I know all about that," the nurse said. "That's how we get her back to normal when she gets disoriented. It's what we call 'reality orientation.'"

That made my day. My heart was rejoicing. As I was about to leave the building, I stopped at the front desk. I was so excited I just had to share this good news.

"Tell me," I said to the aide on duty," Do you know any portion of Scriptures?"

"No, I'm afraid not."

"Well, then Audie is better off than you are—right?"

The aide thought that was funny and started to laugh.

"It really isn't funny. You ought to start reading and memorizing the Scriptures so that when you get old you'll have something on which to fall back."

"You're probably right. You might have something there."

I turned to leave when the aide said in a more serious vein, "It truly is a miracle, isn't it?"

"Yes, it is. I've learned that the spirit is stronger than the flesh. What we store up in our hearts, pertaining to godliness, will benefit us all the days of our lives."

Looking Back

My attitude has completely changed about visiting nursing homes. I used to go to give of myself and I guess that is still true to a point—but I receive so much more than I ever give.

God has given me a special privilege— the privilege of having shared in the lives of a few people in their twilight years.

Can a person be a witness in a nursing home? . . . You bet!

15

What Would You Have Said—

When Someone Wanted Both Jesus and Buddha as His God?

Loo Kim and Ghigi

I opened the door, and the young man standing on my porch greeted me with a broad smile.

"I'm Loo Kim," he said. "My mother sent me to see you. She wants you to talk to me."

I invited this tall, handsome Korean teenager to come in. I figured he was about seventeen years old and close to six feet tall. As most Orientals, he had jet-black hair.

I had never seen him before but I was expecting him. I liked him instantly.

Loo's mother was in my Bible class. She had been a Christian for about a year. She was concerned for her teenage son.

"He is a very rebellious young man. I have been sending

110

him to some very wise men for counseling but he refuses to go anymore."

"They don't help me," he said.

"Well, then, you *must* go to see my American Bible-study teacher. You need some wise counsel, and maybe she can help you," his mother said.

To my surprise, Loo was willing to come to my home. There was no formal introduction. His mother just dropped him off at the street, and he came to the door by himself.

"I give you a lot of credit for coming to see me," I said. "I'm not so sure my son would be willing to talk to a woman he had never met before."

"I really don't mind," he answered.

I have watched many times with great interest, the respect the Orientals have for their elders. I admire it. We, as Americans, can learn much from them.

We sat down and talked about generalities for a while. Then he said, "I had thought about becoming a doctor, but I've looked into it and I think it's going to take too much of my time. I intend to enjoy life and have some fun."

"You're about ready to graduate from high school. What are your intentions? Will you go to college?" I asked.

"Oh, yes, my grades are very good. I have no problems with my studies. I plan to go to the University of Michigan, but I want to take some courses that leave me a lot of free time," he responded.

"What about God in your life?" I asked. "Have you ever accepted Jesus Christ as your Savior?"

"No, I haven't. We were all Buddhists in our family, but my mother has become a Christian. She's told me all about Christianity and would like me to become a believer in Jesus Christ, too."

"What is keeping you from becoming a believer?" I asked.

"Well, if heaven would open up and I would see God, I would believe."

111

"That will never happen Loo," I said. "The Bible says that '. . . The righteous will live by faith" (Rom. 1:17).

"How does a person get faith?" he asked.

"The Bible says in Romans 10:17 'Faith comes from hearing the message, and the message is heard through the word of Christ.' In other words you learn about God and Jesus Christ, who is God in the flesh, by reading his Word. The Bible is God's Word," I said. "Would you be willing to read the Book of John and then in a couple of weeks come back, and we'll discuss what you've read?"

"I would be happy to do that."

I was delighted with his response.

Exactly two weeks later, Loo called and wanted to come over. When he arrived, he announced that he had not only read the Book of John but also Matthew and Luke.

"It was fascinating," he said.

I was encouraged with his interest. He seemed eager to learn.

"Do you know that Jesus Christ came to earth for the very purpose of dying on the cross for our sins? That he actually was our substitute? We deserved to die but he took our place? Let me read to you what the Bible says in John 3:16. 'For God so loved the world that he gave his one and only Son, that whoever believes in him shall not perish but have eternal life.'

"To be in the family of God, you have to receive Jesus Christ as your personal Savior. The Bible says that in John 1:12: 'Yet to all who received him [Jesus Christ], to all who believed in his name '[that means, all that he stands for],' he gave the right to become the children of God.'"

"You have given me a lot to think about," he said, "I'd like to talk again."

We had many talks before he left for the University of Michigan. Each time I felt he got a little closer to understanding what Christianity was all about.

One day I said, "Loo, do you understand what it means to be a Christian?"

"Yes, I feel that I do."

"Would you like to receive Jesus Christ as your personal Savior?"

"Yes, I would," was his answer.

I helped him pray. He confessed that he was a sinner, and said he would like to receive Jesus Christ as his God.

Of course I was delighted. Loo came to church with me the week before he left for college. I introduced him to some of the young people. He seemed happy to get acquainted with other Christians.

The disappointment came a short time later when he announced to his mother that even though he had become a Christian, he was still a Buddhist. He had just added Jesus Christ to his list of gods.

His mother was greatly disappointed, and I was devastated. I had never had an experience like that!

I discovered that I had a lot to learn. The Oriental culture is different from ours. It is natural for them to have many gods.

I will be better prepared the next time, I thought.

The next time came a few months ago when I was in Florida. I had been asked to counsel a Chinese woman. She had responded to the pastor's invitation to receive Jesus Christ as her Savior.

After our introductions, I asked, "Ghigi, "what is your religious background?"

"I'm a Buddhist, but I want to receive Jesus as my God."

"If you receive Jesus as your God," I said, "he has to be your only God. You cannot have Buddha as your God any longer. Are you willing to do that?"

She hesitated briefly and then said, "Yes, I am."

"Do you have any idols in your home?" I asked.

"Yes, I do. I have three."

"You will have to get rid of them. You cannot have Jesus Christ and your idols too," I said.

"I see that my Christian friend has much joy and happiness. I do not have that. She says that Jesus makes the difference."

"Yes, Jesus Christ does make a difference in a person's life. You see there is much joy when we realize that he died on the cross for our sins. He took the penalty we deserved, and we are free. He takes our guilt, and we have peace. I call that God's loving exchange. That is why the real Christian has joy in his heart."

I told her the story of Loo, and said, "You see now why you cannot have two gods? The Bible says, 'Thou shalt have no other gods before me.'"

"Yes, I want Jesus as my only God."

She bowed her head, confessed she had sinned against God and received Jesus Christ as her personal Savior and Lord.

I was glad her friend was with her. She would disciple her and help her to understand the Scriptures better.

I met my Chinese friend a week later at a restaurant. My husband suggested that I ask her if she got rid of her idols.

I approached her and asked, "Ghigi, have you gotten rid of your idols yet?"

"Yes, I destroyed the idols I had in my house. But I had a gold necklace that had an idol on it. It was very expensive. I gave it to my friend. She is a Buddhist. I didn't want to waste the money."

"Are you going to tell your friend about Jesus Christ?" I asked.

"Yes, I already have."

"What will she do with the necklace when she accepts Jesus Christ as *her* Savior?"

"Oh, I hadn't thought about that," she exclaimed. We all laughed. She got the point. She was just a beginner. She will learn.

Looking Back

The Eastern religions are not the only ones who do not believe Jesus is God in the flesh. Many religions in America have good things about them, but unless they believe that Jesus Christ is God they are a cult and a false religion. We need to be on guard that we are not deceived. We need to know the Word of God so we can help these deluded people.

The Bible is our only source of truth. The person we witness to must know we are not presenting our own ideas or opinions but the teachings of the Scriptures. The Bible is the only place we can learn anything about God or Jesus Christ.

Another young friend of mine was invited to a study group. It was called "The Making of Miracles." He wasn't sure what they were studying but he brought his Bible.

As they began discussing miracles, my friend brought out his Bible and referred to a particular Scripture verse. In disgust one member of the group ordered, "Put that book away. We don't believe that stuff."

My friend couldn't stay for the rest of the meeting. "I would be compromising my stand for the Lord," he said.

We all need to take a *stand* for the Lord Jesus. We need to let people know that our first allegiance is to our Savior, the Lord Jesus Christ and that we can have "no other gods before him."

16

What Would You Have Said—

When the Person You Were Talking to Emphasized Tongues and Healing Above Salvation?

Carla

"I would like a separate bill for this Scotch tape. It doesn't go with the rest of the order," I said as I proceeded to put the other twenty items on the counter.

It looked kind of silly all by itself. I laughed and said, "It's only forty-nine cents, but I do get a tax credit because it's for my business. Every penny counts when it's tax time."

"What kind of business do you have?" the cashier asked.

"Actually I don't have a business. I have written a book, and there are expenses connected with it. I have to keep books which show profit and loss and, of course, expenses."

"What is the name of your book?"

"It's called *What Do You Say When* . . . It's about sharing the gospel of Jesus Christ."

I looked at her to see if she understood. I was rewarded with a smile.

"I know what you're talking about. I have been raised in church and Sunday school and have always been taught that we should share our faith. But my husband and his family place more emphasis on the healing of the body than on sharing the gospel. That's all they talk about."

"We all want to be healed of our illnesses. No one enjoys being sick," I commented.

The cashier seemed interested and since there was no one behind me waiting to be served, I continued. "Jesus healed many sick people. He also fed multitudes who were hungry. Do you remember what happened after that?" I asked.

"I can't recall."

"The crowds lost track of Jesus for a while and when they found him again they asked, '. . . When did you get here?' (John 6:25). Jesus knew their hearts and said, '. . . you are looking for me, not because you saw miraculous signs but because you ate the loaves and had your fill' (v. 26).

"The people were using Jesus for what they could get out of him. They wanted physical satisfaction. They were not interested in Jesus for himself, only what he could give them.

"When the emphasis is on the temporal rather than the spiritual, we're out of alignment with God. The reason Jesus came was, '. . . to seek and to save what was lost' [Luke 19:10]. That's primary. That's what the gospel is all about. We do need to minister to the sick and to pray for them. The Bible says, 'As we have opportunity, let us do

117

good to all people, especially to those who belong to the family of believers' [Gal. 6:10]. But the greatest need of a human being is to know Jesus Christ as personal Savior."

"That really makes sense," she said. "Where can I get your book?"

"The bookstores are just beginning to get them. They can order one for you."

"Don't you have any with you?"

"Well, yes, the publisher sent me the first copies. I do have some in the car."

"I'm just about ready to go on my break. Would you be willing to wait for me and let me have a copy of your book? I feel it would be a great help to me."

I waited a few minutes, and off we went to the car. She seemed excited and enthusiastic.

"I can hardly wait to start reading it," she said. "By the way, my name's Carla. I'm so glad we met today. Please stop and see me when you come back to the store."

Two weeks later I had occasion to visit K-Mart for some purchases. I looked for Carla and waited until she was free.

"Have you had a chance to browse through my book yet?" I asked.

She looked at me with a big smile and said, "You won't believe this but your book has changed our marriage."

"How is that?" I asked.

"Remember our discussion? I told you that my husband and his family placed the greatest emphasis on the healing of the body rather than healing the sin in our lives? Because we differed so much in our understanding of the Scriptures, we grew further and further apart. I suggested to my husband that we read your book together. He was so excited about God's saving power displayed in the people you led to Christ that he has a new zeal to be a witness for Christ. We are together in this. It has cemented our marriage. He now realizes that Jesus commanded believers to be witnesses. It's not an option for us any longer."

Looking Back

Jesus said, "Come, follow me, and I will make you fishers of men" (Matt. 4:19). There are many ways we can fish for souls. First, we release the bait and then wait to see if there is a tug on the line. My bait was a roll of Scotch tape. I needed it for my business. A woman's natural curiosity caused her to ask, "What kind of a business do you have?" She took the bait.

I didn't know what Carla's need was but God did, and he directed our conversation. Yes, she already knew Jesus Christ as her personal Savior, but her marriage was not honoring to the Lord. Their household was divided. They needed to put Second Timothy 2:15 into practice: "Do your best to present yourself to God as one approved, a workman who does not need to be ashamed and who correctly handles the word of truth."

We are admonished in Ephesians 4:2, 3: "Be completely humble and gentle; be patient, bearing with one another in love. Make every effort to keep the unity of the Spirit through the bond of peace."

17

What Would You Have Said—

When You Discovered the Subtlety of Evil Influences?

My husband and I stopped at a rest area on Interstate 96 one day. A woman about thirty-five years old came in, singing something about the greatest love. Her four year-old daughter came happily bouncing along beside her.

"What's the name of the song you're singing?" I asked.

"It's called 'No Greater Love.'"

"I know something about *that* love," I said. "You're singing about God's love, right?"

"Oh, no, I'm singing about self-love."

I was really surprised. "But the greatest love is God's love."

"Oh, no, you can't love anyone until you first love yourself," she said.

Mmm, I thought, *this is the world's answer to the poor self-image problem. They've got the cart before the horse.*

"I'm afraid I can't agree with you," I said. "You see, when you understand God's love and the price he paid to forgive your sin by sending Jesus Christ to die in your place, only then can you love yourself. You must be worth a lot to God since he was willing to send his Son to die on the cross for you. The greatest love beyond question has to be God's love."

"Well . . ."she said thoughtfully, "I've never thought about it that way before."

Her little girl began tugging at her mother's dress, and they were on their way.

I wanted to give the woman something to think about and I pray someone else will water the seed that was sown. She needs to be a good role model for her daughter. Only the truth of God can accomplish that.

Before the evening news came on, I listened to a commercial.

"You all know happiness is lots of money in the bank, food on the table, and of course the right kind of tires on your car. That all adds up to security in life," the TV announcer proclaimed.

Daily we get bombarded with lies from the media. We are told what kind of cars to buy, slacks to wear, cereals to eat, cosmetics to use, and so forth. Generally it is not based on the merit of the product but by the sexy young men or women who are used to enhance it. (So the advertisers think.)

Most of us try to ignore these ads, and some feel the commercials are perfectly harmless. In a subtle way, however, they have their influence. The advertisers have our eyes and ears. All they need to do is to pressure us and tempt us to loosen our purse strings.

I began to wonder, *Am I easily influenced?*

That evening, my next-door neighbor, Sheila, and I walked over to our vegetable garden.

"It looks like you got yourself some new tennis shoes," I said.

121

"No, they're not new; I just washed them."

"I'm wearing the same brand. What a difference," I said. "I was thinking about getting some new ones. Maybe I should try washing mine first."

I was pleasantly surprised when after applying a little soap and water, and of course a brush, my shoes looked as new as Sheila's.

I showed my newly scrubbed shoes to my husband.

"Wow, what a difference a little cleaning makes," he remarked.

A few days later, I noticed my husband's shoes out on the porch drying. He too had been influenced.

I became more acutely aware that there are good and bad influences in life. I was discussing this with my friend Ola one day.

"It's interesting, you should mention that," she said. "I've been thinking about the same thing lately.

"My little three-year-old granddaughter," she said, "was sitting in the backseat of our car when I heard her cry out, 'Oh, oh, oh, my!'"

"What's the matter, Audie?" she asked.

"My nail polish doesn't match the color of my outfit," she said in a very distressed tone of voice.

From a three-year-old, that was funny. Where did she get the idea? From her mother, of course.

I had watched my *own* three-year-old granddaughter, Annie, do an imitation of her mom. She was staying with me for a few days. She seemed so proud of her new purse. I noticed she would take out a tube of chapstick and apply it to her lips, then she smeared it on her cheeks. She put it back in her purse only to take it out again and repeat the process over and over again.

Finally I asked, "Annie, what are you doing?"

"I'm putting capstick on my yips and my keeks, Gramma."

"You mean your lips and your cheeks, don't you?"

122

"Yes, Gramma," she said impatiently, "I'm putting it on my yips and my keeks."

She wanted to be a grown-up like her mom.

Children learn to imitate early in life. It's rather scary when we think about it.

I began to realize what an awesome responsibility we, as mothers and grandmothers, have toward our children.

I think the first time I became keenly aware of how my behavior affected my children was when I heard my oldest daughter, Karen, scolding her doll.

"Now, you just behave yourself. If you don't, I'll put you right to bed." She shook her little finger at the doll as she was speaking. "And if you're not good, there won't be any treats today either."

Dear me, that sounds just like me, I thought. It made me realize the responsibility I had in raising my children. What I said, and how I said it, would be imitated by my children. How else do they learn?

Being a grandmother is different. We don't need to do much scolding or disciplining. We can leave that to the parents. Romans 5:3,4 says, ". . . we also rejoice in our sufferings [tribulations], for we know that suffering brings perseverance [patience]; perseverance, character; and character, hope." We experienced tribulation with our children to prepare us to be more patient as grandparents. We tease about being able to love them and leave them. Grandchildren are wonderful, and we do have a responsibility to be good role models.

I watched my four-year-old granddaughter leave her seat and walk down the aisle toward the platform of the church. She hesitated, and then walked up the steps to the podium and stood right next to the speaker. I was the speaker for the mother-and-daughter banquet of her parents' church. I had to make a choice quickly. Should I send her back to her seat and tell her she did not belong on the platform—or what should I do? With an automatic impulse I put my arm around her shoulder and kept on talking. She stood quietly beside me until I had finished. Then she looked up at me and said, "Gramma, I just wanted to be with you."

I will never forget that experience. (I'm glad I didn't send her back to her seat!)

Annie's twelve years old now and is still willing to listen to what I have to say. We're great friends. I was amazed and pleasantly surprised when her mother told me she was interested in reading her grandmother's writings on evangelism. She's old enough to understand what it's all about, and has accepted Jesus Christ as her Savior. She is growing as a Christian.

Annie is the oldest of three girls. Her two sisters look to her for leadership.

Each one of the girls have their own separate bedrooms. One night Ruthie, her ten-year-old sister, had a nightmare and woke up crying. Annie got out of bed to see what was troubling her.

"What's wrong, Ruthie?" she asked.

"I had a terrible dream about the program I saw on television today. It was about saying *no* to drugs. They showed the needle drug addicts use and the terrible things that happen when people take drugs. I've been thinking about it all day, and it's really scary. That's what I was dreaming about."

As Ruthie continued to cry, Annie said, "Let's pray about it. God will help you. Then it will be okay." As Annie was praying, their mother came up the stairs and waited quietly until they were finished. Then Annie said, "Maybe God allowed you to watch the program so you could see what happens to people who take drugs. Then you won't be tempted when someone comes along and offers them to you."

Annie may only be twelve years old but she knew how to help her sister. She didn't say, "Oh, it's only a dream. It really didn't happen." She went to the God of all comfort. She had confidence he would help.

Because someone was a good influence in Annie's life, she in turn was able to be a good role model to her sister. It doesn't matter if we are young or old, we influence the behavior of those we are around. Whether it be for good or bad. Just think, at any age we can be God's tool for helping others. What a privilege!

The world is screaming its lies at us every day. "Look, and taste, it's good," it says. "Then you'll discover what you're missing." It's no different today than it was for Eve in the Garden. She took a look, lusted, and then tasted. Then it was too late. As Christians we need to be discerning, lest we get trapped in Satan's clutches.

We also need to be in constant prayer for our loved ones. We need to pray not only for our children, grandchildren, and our friends, but for those we have opportunity to influence for the Lord.

Looking Back

As I look back I realize there is a certain chain of influence. We influence our children, our children influence their friends. Annie may be young but she influenced her sister to pray and talk to God when a problem arose. We can encourage children to do this. I remember the first time I apologized to my son. "I'm sorry, Tim. I was unfair. I was unduly hard on you. Will you forgive me?"

"Aw, it's okay, Mom," he said.

I discovered after that, it was much easier for him to admit his faults to me.

I often say, "I wish I had done things differently. If only I knew then what I know now I'd have been a better mother.

God didn't make us mothers in our old age. He gave us children when we were young, when we had the energy and capacity to take care of them. Yes, we make mistakes but we can learn from them. We can learn to forgive and to love as the Father forgives and loves us, and be a positive influence on others.

18

What Would You Have Said—

When a Person Found That "Things" Don't Satisfy?

Kelly

I met Kelly one Sunday morning in the counseling room at the church. She had responded to the pastor's invitation to be available to God for witnessing. She gave me her name, and I told her my name was Nellie Pickard.

Kelly had a surprised look on her face. She hesitated a moment, then said, "Nellie Pickard? Are you the author of the book *What Do You Say When* . . . the book on witnessing?"

"Yes, I am," I answered.

Pat started to laugh. "You won't believe it but that book is one of the reasons I came forward this morning."

"Tell me about it," I said.

"I'm a rather new Christian," she said. "I loved reading

your book. It really challenged me, but I felt I could never witness effectively to anyone because I don't know the Bible like you do. You seem to witness so easily and naturally."

"God doesn't expect you to witness like I do. No two people ever have the same testimony. But if you are willing, he'll bring people to you who need to hear what God has done in your life. You needn't be fearful. God's in control, you know."

"I can hardly believe it," she said, as she reached over and gave me a hug. "To think God put us together this morning is incredible. Thank you for writing the book."

"I wrote the book hoping God would use it to motivate Christians to witness," I said. "You have no idea how you have encouraged me this morning. Isn't God good to allow us to see some of the fruits of our labor?

"You said my book was one of the reasons you responded to the invitation this morning. What did the pastor say that caused you to come forward?" I asked.

"When he said, 'Lost opportunities can never be retrieved,' I couldn't help but think that someone went out of their way to speak to me about Christ. When he said, 'God wants you to take the opportunities he gives you to share the gospel with others,' I felt that was meant for me. Between the book I read and the sermon this morning, I decided to take another step of faith. I made a commitment to be a witness for the Lord," she said.

"Tell me, Kelly," I said, "how did you become a Christian?"

She smiled, "I was a very unhappy person. I could have just about anything money could buy. One day I looked at my beautiful house, my car and my lovely wardrobe. *'What's wrong with me? I* asked myself. *Why am I so unhappy?'* I sat down, and for the first time in my life I prayed seriously to the Lord: 'Dear Lord, help me out of my misery. Something is very wrong in my life. Please send someone to show me the way.'

"I meant every word of my prayer," she said, "I wanted to know the truth and God answered. About an hour later, a neighbor came to my door, and invited me to a Bible study. 'I can't believe you're here, I said, 'I just prayed and asked God to help me out of my misery. Here you are in answer to my prayer.'

"My neighbor introduced me to Jesus Christ, the way, the truth and the life. I received him that day as my personal Savior. I now know what the abundant life is all about. It certainly isn't in things but in Christ."

There was an air of excitement about Kelly as she said, "I really do want to be a witness for Jesus Christ. I want to be available to him."

"Perhaps you can get involved in the 'Evangelism Explosion' group. They call every Monday night on the people that have visited the church. It will be a wonderful way to learn to share the gospel with a stranger. You observe someone else share at first, and then when you are ready, you get a chance to share. The training is excellent," I said.

We prayed together and then we both left. She left happy about her new commitment to Christ. I went home rejoicing because of the opportunity I had to encourage a new believer in Christ.

Looking Back

Christians need Christians! As the body of Christ, each one of us can contribute to the needs of another believer. In the case of Kelly, God met her need when she called on him for help. He provided a Christian neighbor. The neighbor showed her that it was normal for her to feel dissatisfied. *Things* can never satisfy the longing of the soul. Only Jesus Christ can meet that need.

After growing in the Christian life for a while, God provided a challenge for Kelly. She understood that the gift of salvation was not something for her to keep only for herself. It was to be shared. Her problem was one of timidity. "I don't know the Bible very well. I'm afraid I won't do a good job," she said.

The longer we live the Christian life, the more we realize that God is in control. He brings people into our lives that he wants us to minister to. Some need to accept Jesus Christ as Savior. Others may need discipling. Some may just need encouragement to live for the Lord. All of us can share what Jesus Christ has done for us. We don't need to be theologians to do this.

We have learned from Kelly's story that God met her need when she was ready, when her heart was prepared to receive Jesus as her Savior.

When she had walked with him for a while, the Spirit of God nudged her to be his witness. She struggled with that for a while and yet in God's mercy he brought the right circumstances about to encourage her.

There is nothing like the Christian life. It is never boring and it seems as though God has surprises for us every day.

For the Christian, witnessing is not an option. It's a command of the Lord. What he has asked us to do, he will give us the power to follow through. And with it comes joy. It really puts the sparkle into life. Step out in faith and try it!

19

What Would You Have Said—

When a Stranger Invited You to Dinner?

While in church, my husband drew my attention to three people sitting across the aisle. "Have you ever seen them before?" he asked.

"No, I haven't. Let's try to talk to them after the meeting."

Paul and I try to be friendly to visitors. We want them to feel welcome.

Torrey Johnson was speaking on "The Glory of Israel's Future." My eyes kept wandering to the people across the aisle. They kept looking at each other in a strange way. They seemed uncomfortable.

"I wonder if they're Jewish," I whispered to Paul.

"Could be," he answered.

As soon as the "amen" was pronounced in the closing prayer, the three people rushed for the door. They had a distance to go since they had been sitting about halfway down in the auditorium that had a seating capacity of two thousand. I quickly went after them. When I caught up to the younger woman, I tapped her on the shoulder.

"Are you a visitor?" I asked.

"Yes, I am," she answered.

"Did you enjoy the service?"

"Well, I've never heard anything like it and I don't agree with the message," she said.

"I understand," I said. "You're Jewish, right?"

"Yes, I am. My parents and I decided to visit here tonight. We didn't realize it was a church since It looks like a community center from the outside. We saw an ad in the paper which said there was to be a lecture on the 'Future of Israel.' Of course, the speaker is not correct in his assumptions."

"Interesting you should say you are Jewish. I love the Old Testament. In fact I taught the Book of Genesis in a Bible study. I find it fascinating to see how God dealt with his people."

Just then her father came up, waved his arm, and said, "Come on, let's get going." He seemed to be in a hurry.

"Oh, please, don't go." I said, "We're just getting acquainted. Tell me where do you live?"

"We live in Florida in the winter," he replied, "but our home is in New York.

"Do you ever get to Detroit?" I asked.

"Once in a while."

I don't know what made me say it, but I heard it come out of my mouth. "If you ever get to Detroit," I asked, "would you come and have dinner with us?"

"Well, now, aren't you nice!" he exclaimed. "We want *you* to come to *our house* next Friday, six o'clock prompt."

I was overwhelmed. I hardly knew what to say. Refusing was out of the question. After all I had issued the invitation first.

"We'd be delighted to come," I said.

The woman introduced herself as Janice, and said, "This is my father, David Cohen."

132

Before we had a chance to introduce ourselves her mother came to join us.

"This is Mr. and Mrs. . . . ?" She laughed then turned to her mother and said, "Dad's invited these people for dinner next Friday, and we don't even know their names."

Her mother looked surprised but responded, "How lovely. We'll certainly look forward to your visit."

"Our name is Pickard, Paul and Nellie. I didn't get your mother's name."

"Mom's name is Rachel," Janice said, as we shook hands.

"My husband is a rabbi," Janice said with a twinkle in her eyes. "He'll set you straight." Even though she was teasing, I felt she meant it.

"That will be exciting," I said as I gulped. "I've never met a rabbi before. I'd love to talk to him and pick his brain."

On the way home I turned to Paul and said, "*Wow*, I wonder where this will lead us?"

"I think it will be very interesting," he said.

During the following week both Paul and I prayed much for the coming event. We asked God for wisdom and that he would love these dear people through us.

Friday evening came and I must admit I was a bit nervous. We arrived promptly at 6:00 P.M. Janice came to the door and graciously invited us in. We were introduced to three other couples. They seemed friendly and made us feel at home.

The men then departed to the closed-in porch on the opposite side of the house. The women stayed in the living room.

It wasn't long before the women started to talk about their disappointment in a certain TV personality. "She used to be one of my favorite talk-show hosts, but lately her language is so smutty I can't stand listening to her," one of the women said. "I'm thinking of writing her a letter and telling her I thought she was above the smut and dirt of the media. I'd like her to know I'm disappointed in her."

Mmm, I thought, *these women have high standards. I like that.*

Janice leaned over and whispered, "Let's go out on the porch and see what the men are doing." She seated me right next to her husband.

"Aaron," Janice said, "Nellie says she wants to 'pick your brain.'"

The rabbi looked interested. "What would you like to know?" he asked.

"I am interested in knowing how you conduct your services. Do you preach a sermon like our minister does? As a rabbi what is your procedure?"

"We usually have a discussion. I may ask a question like, 'Do you believe the Bible is true, and is it relevant in our lives today?'"

"That sounds interesting," I said, "I believe the Bible is true, and it certainly is relevant in our lives today. Humans are still as rebellious as they were in Bible times."

"How would you handle the story of Cain and Abel?" I asked.

"We would discuss rebellion and how it affects us."

"What about the fact that Cain didn't bring the proper sacrifice? It was supposed to be a blood sacrifice."

I had not been aware until then that all the men in the room were listening. By the expression on their faces it was apparent that they were keenly interested in what was going on.

"What makes you so interested in the Jews?" a man named Isidore asked. He seemed rather belligerent.

At that point, my husband spoke up. "I'm glad you asked. On the way over here tonight, Nellie and I were talking about the fact that the Oracles of God were given to the Jews. Also, almost every book in the New Testament was written by a Jew. We owe them a great debt."

"Oh, well now, I never thought about that," Isidore said. "But we don't believe in those bloody sacrifices."

"Then you don't know your Bible very well," I teased.

"She's right," the rabbi told the group. Then he turned to me and with a smile said, "We usually don't let Isidore speak, but since you're here, he's taking advantage." Everyone laughed.

We all chatted for a while. Everyone seemed to be in a good mood. Then Mrs. Cohen came in the room and handed each man, including my husband, a yarmulke (a little black skull cap the Jews wear to show reverence to God).

Paul's hair gets quite curly in the Florida weather. When he put the yarmulke on I thought, *My husband would make a very handsome Jew.*

We were all invited to a beautifully set table. The food had been prepared ahead of time. Since Friday night is the beginning of the Sabbath, no cooking is allowed.

The attention was focused on us. We were different. We were outsiders. It was understandable. Since I was the one who had been asking the rabbi questions, others were eager to get in on the conversation.

Rachel, the rabbi's mother-in-law asked, "Tell us about your children. Do they believe as you do?"

Before I could reply, Isidore (the man who didn't believe in a bloody sacrifice) interrupted and said, "If you're born into a Jewish family, you'll always be a Jew. If you're born into a Christian family, you'll always be a Christian."

"Not necessarily so," I said.

"Well, then how does a person become a Christian?" he asked.

"If I tell you, I have to mention Jesus Christ, and I don't want to offend you."

"You may mention Jesus Christ as long as we ask you. But not if you initiate it," Janice said.

"Well, then, I'll tell you how a person becomes a

Christian. Someone may be born into a Christian home but they are not born a Christian. Everyone is born a sinner. God's standards are perfect. No one can reach them.

"God provided a way that we could be accepted by him. Each individual must confess he or she is a sinner in the sight of a holy God. That is not enough, however; each must receive Jesus Christ as his or her personal Savior. Jesus Christ is our perfect sacrifice. He was without spot or blemish and willingly bore the penalty of our sins on the cross.

"The Bible also says if you confess with your mouth that "Jesus is Lord" and believe in your heart that God raised him from the dead you will be saved (Rom. 10:9).

"I have done that and Paul has too. It doesn't mean we never sin again. We are human and we have learned to hate sin because of what it cost our Savior, Jesus Christ. When we sin in word or deed and become aware of it, we confess it to God and he forgives us.

"I was born into a Christian home and was taught all of this. For many years I took all my teaching for granted. I didn't appreciate what Jesus Christ had done for me. It didn't affect my life. I had head knowledge but now I've made a personal commitment to Jesus Christ. He is my Savior and Lord. It's changed my life. I'm a new person. I now want to live for him and please him.

"My children experienced the same thing. They weren't sure what Mom and Dad taught them was what they wanted. They did a little experimenting on their own but found out that Jesus Christ was the only answer to life.

"Not only has my life been changed but I have seen the change in many other lives as well," I added.

The rabbi turned to me and said, "If what you believe changes people's lives for the better, then what you believe is valid."

"I was born in England," Rachel said. "As a young person the kids in the neighborhood called me a 'Jesus killer.' It made me feel awful. They wouldn't play with me."

"It was our sins that sent him to the cross. He was willing to die on the cross for our sins. You need to know not all people who call themselves Christians are true believers. You see, God said, 'I will bless those who bless you [referring to the Jews] and whoever curses you I will curse . . .'" (Gen. 12:3).

"Well, we asked you to tell us about Christianity and you did. Thank you." Rachel said.

It seemed as though the air was cleared. The questions everyone had seemed to be answered for the time being.

We spent a pleasant evening but then it was getting late and people began to leave.

"Before I leave, Aaron, I want to ask you who you think Isaiah is writing about in the fifty-third chapter?"

"I'm not familiar with that Scripture but I'll look it up and tell you the next time we see you."

As we were walking out the door, one woman who had recently returned from Hungary came up to me and whispered, "My grandmother told me about Jesus and taught me to pray."

"I'm so glad," I said. There was no opportunity to talk further.

Mr. and Mrs. Cohen walked us to the car and talked to us for a long time. "We will be leaving for New York next week but when we come back next year, we must get together," Rachel said.

"The next time, you must come to our home," I urged.

By the time we finally left it was 1:30 A.M. We generally retire around 11:00 P.M. On the way home, Paul and I talked about the freedom we were given to share the gospel. "To think they would ask us to tell them about our faith," I said. "To me, that's amazing."

It was early morning before I could settle down to sleep.

The stimulus of the previous evening kept me awake. We had had a good time. We thanked God for the beautiful experiences he is pleased to give us.

One of the first things I thought of when we returned to Florida the following year was, *I must call my new Jewish friends and invite them over.* I was anxious to know if Rabbi Aaron had read the fifty-third chapter of Isaiah and what his conclusions were.

When Rachel answered the phone, I asked if all four of them could come over the following Thursday evening for dinner.

"I'm not sure about Aaron and Janice, but my husband and I would be delighted. Tell us what time you want us and we'll be there."

"I need to know if there is anything you should not eat. I'll be careful to serve the proper food," I said.

"Why don't you just serve dessert this time; then there won't be a problem."

I was disappointed when Aaron, the rabbi, and Janice didn't come. They had previous engagements. Paul and David sat at the dining room table and talked while Rachel and I sat on the sofa. She told me about the trips they had taken abroad and the beautiful things they had brought home with them. Every once in a while she would put her hand on my knee and say, "Nellie, I just love you." She must have done that six times during the evening.

In my heart I said, "Thank you, Lord."

When they started to leave, I expressed my disappointment at not seeing the rabbi and Janice.

"Aaron's going to be chairing a discussion next Saturday at the clubhouse. Maybe you would find it interesting to attend," Rachel said.

I looked at Paul. He nodded so I said, "We'd love to come."

They gave us directions and the time of the meeting.

I could hardly wait for the time to come. When we arrived, there were about a hundred people in the audience.

The rabbi talked about three wise men, the wise men being Pharaoh, his cupbearer, and Joseph. Pharaoh was wise because he told the cupbearer about his dream [Gen. 41]. The cupbearer was wise because he admitted, "This day I remember my shortcomings," and Joseph was wise because he had the smarts.

The rabbi promised that the lecture would end on an upbeat note.

"When I'm finished, we'll have a discussion.

"I can trust a man who remembers his shortcomings," he said, "but I can't trust President————[one of our former presidents] because he didn't remember *his* shortcomings."

As the lecture continued statements were made about Joseph and his intelligence. Then the talk went to the problems in the Near East.

One man raised his hand. "I thought this lecture was going to be upbeat. Frankly I'm scared to death about the happenings in the world. The city I live in hates Jews. I don't like to tell anyone I'm Jewish. As far as I'm concerned, they're all going to be extinguished." Then the man sat down.

I impulsively raised my hand. My heart went out to this group. I will never forget the fear on the faces of the people in that audience. Then I remembered. I was a Christian in a Jewish meeting. I felt I had no right to speak. I quickly put my hand down. Rachel noticed, and to my surprise, took my arm and lifted it—high.

"Nellie's got something to say," she declared.

"Oh, please, I shouldn't have raised my hand. I'm just a visitor. I have no right. Please forgive me."

"If you've got something to say, say it," Rachel offered.

"Nellie, would you like to contribute something?" the rabbi asked.

I quickly turned to my husband. He didn't look at me. I'm sure if he'd found a hole in the floor he would have crawled into it.

Then I realized he would be praying. *He knows how quickly I react,* I thought.

I stood up and explained, "Don't you realize the very fact Jews are alive today is one of the greatest miracles of all time? Remember that God took Abraham and showed him the heavens? He said, 'I will surely bless you and make your descendants as numerous as the stars in the sky and as the sand on the seashore . . . ' [Gen. 22:17; *see also* Gen. 15:5].

"Although President———didn't remember his short-comings, King David remembered *his*. He confessed his sin and God called him 'a man after his own heart . . . ' [1 Sam. 13:14]."

I trembled as I sat down. I was surprised when the people clapped. They seemed delighted that a Christian could remind them of the blessings God had bestowed on the Jews. It calmed their fears.

After the lecture a crowd of people gathered around. One man said, "Thank you for your encouragement. We needed that reminder."

I was both amazed and grateful to God.

David Cohen then announced, "We want you to come to dinner with us. We won't take *no* for an answer."

"We'd love to," I said, "but we are expecting guests from Michigan tomorrow, and I need to do some grocery shopping on the way home tonight," I said.

"There's plenty of time for that," David said. "It's Hanukkah, and we want you to celebrate with us. "Come now, let's get going," he insisted.

It was no use arguing with David, so we went.

When we arrived at their home, the rabbi opened his arms and said, "You sure helped me out today. Thanks a lot."

"I disagree with one thing you said in your lecture," Paul said. "Joseph wasn't wise because he had the smarts. He said God revealed the meaning of the dream to him."

"You're right, Paul, it does say that God revealed it to him. I shouldn't have said that. Thanks for bringing it to my attention."

We looked up the verse later and the exact wording says when Pharaoh sent for Joseph, he said to him, "I had a dream, and no one can interpret it. But I have heard it said of you that when you hear a dream you can interpret it."

"I cannot do it," Joseph replied to Pharaoh, "but God will give Pharaoh the answer he desires" (Gen. 41:15, 16).

It was a privilege to celebrate this special holiday with our Jewish friends. Rabbi explained to us that Hanukkah, which means *dedication,* is called "The Jewish Feast of Lights." It lasts eight days. At sundown on each day a new candle is lit. By the end of the celebration, eight candles stand together.

The feast started about 165 B.C. by Judas Maccabaeus to honor the rededicating of the Jewish temple in Jerusalem. Three years before, a Syrian conqueror had used the temple for idol worship.

This particular evening marked the seventh day of celebration. It was interesting to hear the rabbi pray before the meal. He addressed God as *Adonai* (Lord). The Jew does not address God as we do. The name God is too overwhelming to be expressed or described in words. Too awesome or sacred to be spoken.

He thanked Adonai for his abundant provision and goodness to them. I missed not hearing the prayer end in Jesus' name. *Oh, if only these dear people knew that the veil in the temple has been lifted,* I thought.

After we finished eating there was a knock at the door. A couple we had met earlier at the discussion group came in. Rachel introduced me saying, "Nellie knows the Bible better than any Yiddish woman I know. I mean it, better than *any* Yiddish woman I know. I just love her."

I couldn't believe the love that was shown to us. God had given us a love for each other. I was moved emotionally.

About a month later we were invited to David's eightieth birthday party. The following Sunday after the evening service we went out with the Zondervans, Pat and Mary. I told them about our Jewish friends and the birthday party we were going to attend.

When we got home Pat called and asked, "Will you be up at eight o'clock in the morning? I've got something to give you."

"Yes, we're up before eight."

I wondered what he was up to. Many times in the past he had given us a book or two. When I opened the door the next morning, there stood Pat with a large picture book of Israel. It was in color and had beautiful, breath-taking pictures of the land.

"I want you to give this to your Jewish friend for his birthday," he said.

"You overwhelm me," I said. "What else can I say? I know Mr. Cohen will love it. Thank you. This is what the body of Christ is all about. One fills in where the other one lacks. We didn't know what to get him. This is absolutely perfect."

As we suspected, David loved the gift. It was the second edition of this book. The first book was pictures of Israel but no Scripture was included. Between the time of the first and second edition, both the author and photographer had become Christians and had inserted Scripture verses on each page. It was an exciting gift to give.

When all the gifts had been opened, I went over to the rabbi. I wanted to tell him about my dad.

"My father died since the last time I saw you," I told him. It was beautiful. He died praising the Lord."

"That's remarkable," he observed. "I don't know any people like you. Your faith is beautiful."

As we were talking, Janice came over and handed us a plate.

"Help yourselves to the goodies on the table. There's plenty of food to eat," she said.

I filled my plate and went to look for a place to sit on the porch. Paul sat on the opposite side of the room. There were forty people in attendance. We didn't know any of the guests.

I'm sure it was obvious that Paul and I weren't Jewish. One of women seated near me asked, "How do you know the Cohens? Where did you meet them?"

"They came to a meeting at our church, thinking it was a community center. The speaker was talking about Israel's future, but they didn't agree with the message."

She chuckled. "That's a riot. By the way my name's Betty, and I'm glad you came to the party.

"Rachel tells me you are doing some writing. What do you write about?" she continued.

"People, and their relationship to God."

"Sounds interesting."

She then noticed her empty plate and said to her husband, "Will you please take my plate into the kitchen? Bring me some coffee while you're at it."

Her husband graciously took the plate, and as he left, Betty's friend said, "After twenty-five years, It's time our husbands start waiting on us, don't you think?"

"I couldn't agree more," Betty answered.

I couldn't help it. I had to say something.

"Oh," I said, kiddingly, "who's been bringing home the bacon for the past twenty-five years?"

For a moment there was dead silence. Then they started to laugh. I thought they'd never stop. I finally caught on. Bacon—Jewish? The two don't mix.

I apologized profusely. "I've never used that phrase before—ever. I don't know what made me say it."

"We think it's hilarious. I want you to write that in your book, and I want my name in it. Do you promise?"

"Yes, Betty." (I've kept my promise!)

Sometime after the party, we invited our Jewish friends to our home for dinner. We asked for instruction concerning food.

"Don't serve us any meat or any butter. Fish, fruit, and dessert will be fine."

We had a good time. Our guests all have such a good sense of humor that the evening was without any tension.

After dinner, we got comfortable in the living room. At times everyone would talk at once. It gave me an opportunity to talk to the rabbi.

"Have you had a chance to read the fifty-third chapter of Isaiah?" I asked.

"No, I haven't. Bring me a Bible, and I'll read it right now."

I brought him my Bible and opened it to the text.

After he had finished reading it, I asked, "Who do you think Isaiah is talking about?"

"I think Isaiah is talking about himself," he answered.

"Would you think it strange if I thought Isaiah was talking about Jesus Christ?"

"No, I wouldn't think it was strange. Do you know you are the only one I can talk to about these things?"

Paul kept the rest of the group busy, so we could keep on talking.

It wasn't long before David stood up. "It's time to go. Come on, everybody." As usual, he began waving his arms.

"Go ahead. I'll meet you in the parking lot," the rabbi said.

"We all have to leave together." No one argued with David and so they left.

When we got back to Michigan, we received an invitation to a wedding in their city. When we arrived, we called the Cohens and told them we'd like to see them if it was convenient.

"You must come to dinner," Janice said.

Arrangements were made and we arrived at 6:00 o'clock on Saturday evening. Dinner was ready, and we were seated at a beautifully decorated table. When the rabbi gave thanks for the meal, I recognized quotes from Isaiah. He also used some of the names of God. I commented on it when he had finished.

He beamed as he said, "That was from Isaiah, the sixth chapter. I've been reading that book lately."

We wanted so much to say something about our Lord but we remembered what Janice had said.

"Don't speak about Jesus unless we ask."

It didn't take long before Rachel asked, "Are you a 'Born-Again Christian?'"

"Yes, we are."

"We've discovered 'Born-Again Christians' are different than others who call themselves Christians. We like the 'Born-Again' kind. What makes the difference?" she asked.

"The difference is 'Born-Again Christians' have confessed they are sinners and have received Jesus Christ as their Savior. They then have his Spirit living in them and that affects their behavior. They want to do what's right. They no longer run after sin. They run away from it. They have a natural hunger to know God better," I said.

Everyone was surprised when Rachel quietly said, "I think my father became a 'Born-Again Christian' before he died."

"Her husband turned to her and in a loud voice said, "*He did not.*"

"I was there. I should know," she said.

There was no argument.

We sat at the dining-room table until 10:30 P.M. discussing our faith and God's dealings with the Jews.

"I don't understand why the Jews are called God's chosen people," Janice said. "What were they chosen for?"

"Many Jewish people have asked me that question. The Jew was chosen to carry the Messiah seed and to tell the Gentiles what God is like."

"How can we do that? We don't understand it ourselves."

"Maybe we Christians can help the Jews to know more about God's plan."

The evening ended on that note. There were many hugs and "I love yous" as we left.

Looking Back

We still see our Jewish friends from time to time. It is hard to discuss the Bible with those who are not familiar with Scripture. Even the rabbi knew only the first five books of the Old Testament. He now has started to read other portions. I believe he is searching.

I wrote this chapter to show my readers that witnessing is not just sharing the gospel and then having people sign on the dotted line. We are called to be witnesses. Only God can give the increase. Our job is to be faithful. Some people take years to come to the knowledge of Jesus Christ; others understand in no time at all.

I am not shy about asking anyone if *he* or *she* would like to receive Christ as Savior. I've done that in various situations: on the tennis court, in a swimming pool, or on the porch of our home. With our friends (who I call "David's tribe") it would not have been appropriate. God has given me a sense of timing. The time has not yet come. I, too, must remember that someone else may come and water where I have sown. We leave the results in God's hands.

20

What Would You Have Said—

When She Said, "I Can't Sit Through Class Until You Answer My Questions"?

Dawn

"I've got to ask you some questions before class starts," Dawn pleaded. I had just been introduced to her at our Neighborhood Bible Study. I noticed the woman seemed distraught.

"I won't be able to sit through the session unless I get some answers. I'm desperate. Noreen said you'd be able to help me and invited me to come today. Could we go in another room so we can talk privately?"

I left my coffee cup and roll on a nearby table. Noreen, our hostess, led us to her husband's office.

"When I told you I was desperate, I meant it," Dawn said. "I've got to know how I can get to heaven. What is my part and what is God's part? Who is the Lord and how do I know what truth is?" The words came pouring out of her mouth like a sudden rush of water from a spring. She didn't stop.

"Wait a minute," I said. "One thing at a time."

"It's just that I've gone everywhere for help and I'm about ready to give up. It seems useless. No one seems to know the truth about God."

"There is only one place to find the truth about God and Jesus Christ," I said. "The Bible is the Word of God. It's the only reliable source of truth I know. No one knows anything about God or Jesus Christ apart from the Scriptures."

"Well, then, how can I get to heaven?" she asked.

"First of all I need to ask if you agree with God when he says in Romans 3:23 that 'all have sinned and fall short of the glory of God.' Do you recognize that you, Dawn, have fallen short of God's standards and can't make the grade on your own?"

"I know I'm not good enough." she replied. "Every week I go to confession because I know I have sinned. I try to keep a clean slate but I just can't make it from one week to the next. Fact is, I go to confession on Saturday at 4:00 P.M. and then to Mass on Sunday at 9:00 A.M. I sleep eight hours a night so that doesn't give much time to sin. I thought I might make it to heaven if I died on Sunday right after Mass. I would have fifty-two chances in a year. I just can't take the strain anymore. I feel so empty and hollow on the inside. There's got to be a better way." She put her head in her hands.

"Oh, Dawn," I replied, "there is a better way. Jesus said in John 14:6: 'I am the way, the truth and the life. No one comes to the Father except through me.' You see, Jesus is the way. Let me give you a couple of other verses. Romans 5:6 says, 'Just at the right time, when we were still powerless, Christ died for the ungodly.' The eighth verse says, 'But God demonstrates his own love for us in this: While we were still sinners, Christ died for us.'"

"That's his part," she said. "Now what's my part?"

"Now listen to this, John 1:12 says, 'Yet to all who received him, [Jesus] to those who believed in his name, he gave the right to become the children of God.'"

"Don't I have to do some sort of penance?" she asked.

"Jesus Christ took your penalty. He paid the price for our salvation. We can't work for it. Look, see what it says in Ephesians 2:8, 9. 'For it is by grace you have been saved, through faith—and this not from yourselves, it is the gift of God—not by works, so that no one can boast.' The Scripture goes on to say in the tenth verse: 'For we are God's workmanship, created in Christ Jesus to do good works, which God prepared in advance for us to do.'

"You see, we don't work for our salvation. Jesus Christ is our salvation. But after we have been welcomed into the family of God by accepting Jesus Christ as our Savior, then we show our love for him by doing what pleases him. He shows us his will through his Word, the Bible. It comes supernaturally then, because we have his Spirit living in us.

"If you did penance that means you would be paying the penalty for your sins. That's really an insult to the Savior. He paid the supreme penalty. He gave his life. Now he wants to give you a gift, the gift of salvation and eternal life. Would you like to receive his gift?"

"Oh, yes, with all of my heart."

"Then why don't you tell him that right now?"

There was a strong emotional response as Dawn prayed: "Oh, God, I confess I have sinned over and over again. The horrible part is that I've continually offended Jesus Christ. I'm truly sorry. I want to live for you. Thank you for offering me forgiveness and making a way for me to be accepted by you. I, here and now, receive Jesus Christ as my Savior and Lord. In his name I pray, *Amen*."

Dawn looked at me and said, "Thank you for helping

me today. What a relief. I've been living in torment. I can't believe it's so simple. Now I don't need to strive any longer. I can come to these Bible studies and learn more about Jesus."

The women in the other room were patiently waiting for us to return and start the study. I shared with them what had happened. They were excited as they expressed their joy about Dawn's decision to follow Christ. Some of the women knew why Dawn and I had a private conversation and had been praying for us.

Dawn loved the Bible studies and was growing in love and knowledge of the Scriptures. She was eating it up.

I was surprised when she announced one day, "I've decided I'm not going to go to church anymore. I've been to all kinds of churches, and each one confuses me more than the previous one. I'm only going to come to this Bible study. It's really all I need."

"Why don't you come to my church?" I asked. I know you'll love our pastor. You say you love the Bible study. I guarantee you'll love his preaching even more.

"I don't know." She hesitated then she said, "I'm really satisfied just coming to the Bible study. I work on my lesson each week and I'm really getting a lot out of it."

"What about your children? What kind of teaching are they getting? I asked.

"I know you're right. I must see to it that they get good teaching." She then turned and looked directly into my eyes and said, "You think we'll like it, huh?" She gave me a skeptical look.

"It won't hurt you to try," I answered. "How about next Sunday?"

"I suppose you won't let me come back to the Bible class if I don't come," she said.

"Of course I will. That has nothing to do with it. You don't have to come. I just think it will meet a need in your life and that of your children," I said.

150

"Okay, I'll see what the children say. I've got a couple in high school. I hope I can persuade them."

Dawn's husband was gone a great deal of the time. His business kept him away most of the week. He chose not to attend the service. The following Sunday Dawn and her children came to church. As I arrived, I noticed them sitting at the front of the church. They were actually sitting in the second row. *My, they're brave to sit this close to the speaker their very first visit,* I thought.

Before I could ask her how she enjoyed the service she walked over to me and said, "I know this is where I belong. This is it for me. I've never heard such a wonderful sermon before—ever," she declared.

"Joe Stowell is truly a man of God," I replied. "You'll learn a lot sitting under his ministry."

Dawn's children weren't as happy about the service as their mother, but she told them they must attend church with her.

It wasn't long before Peter, her oldest son, became acquainted with some of the young people at the church. He joined in their activities and soon became a part of it.

Peter recently told me that the first two Sundays at church he hated it. "It just wasn't for me," he said. "I really didn't listen to the sermon. My mind kept wandering. I was confused. I had so many problems, I just wanted to get away from everything. I thought if I could just start life over again maybe I could make it. I was attending Cranbrook Academy [a private boys' school]. Anyone should be grateful to be able to attend there, but I wasn't happy.

"One of the young people from the church invited me to a retreat. I decided to go, and there, under the ministry of Dawson McAllister, my eyes were opened. I made a conscious choice to follow Jesus Christ.

"It took a year though, before I realized that every Christian has a responsibility to share the Good News of the gospel. It was made clear to me at another retreat I attended.

"Joe Stowell, our pastor was speaking. His message hit hard. 'Are you satisfied with being just another Christian in a pew?' he asked. 'Or do you want to go all the way with the Lord? Do you really want to live for him?'

"I said to myself, *I'm either going all the way or not at all.* That is when I told the Lord, 'I'm not going to play at being a Christian. I'm ready to take that responsibility. I want to be a witness for you.'"

I was delighted to hear Peter's story. I couldn't help but think, *If Dawn hadn't taken her family to church that first Sunday morning Peter might not be telling me this wonderful story.*

"Have you had many opportunities to witness for the Lord?" I asked Peter.

"After my commitment to be a witness for Jesus Christ," he said, "I had an opportunity to go to New York City with some young people from the church to do street evangelism. There I had many openings to witness. I talked to the rich, the poor, and to people from other countries. There are so many needy people in New York. Many people responded to the gospel message. It was a wonderful experience.

"I had the mistaken idea that it was mostly the poor people that we should try to reach for Christ," he went on. "The rich didn't seem to have any needs. I soon discovered that the rich had just as many problems—different perhaps—but problems nevertheless. It's just that they didn't show their hurts on the outside. I got close to a few and found once they were willing to talk, they too were hurting. They were people needing the peace and forgiveness only Jesus Christ can give.

"I had been home only two days," Peter said, "when I was asked if I'd like to go to Guatemala with a team of young people from the church. I didn't have much time to get ready but I jumped at the chance. There we helped missionaries. We painted and repaired whatever needed fixing. We did whatever we could to ease the load of the missionaries. I gained a lot of insight as to the work of missionaries. Our Spanish was marginal but we had a chance to pass out tracts. We tried to communicate the love of Christ by our attitude toward them."

"What have you been doing since you graduated from high school?" I asked.

"I've had a desire for a long time to climb Mount McKinley. A couple of years ago the opportunity came. I had the privilege of going with a group. One of the team members was a Christian. Between the two of us we witnessed to every member of the team.

"Now I have a chance to go to Kenya and to climb Mount Kilimanjaro," Peter went on. "I'm going with the National Outdoor Leadership School. We will be learning camping skills and survival training. There will be sixteen people in our group. Everything that happens is dependent on the cooperation of each individual member."

"How long will you be gone?" I asked.

"We'll be gone three months. It will also include a safari and time spent with some tribespeople hunting and fishing."

"It sounds exciting," I said. "Do you know any of the other team members?"

"No, I don't know anyone. I am praying though, that God will send another Christian on the trip. I want to be a witness for the Lord while I'm there. It would be nice to have another believer along whose mind-set is the same as mine. Then we could work together."

"I'll be eager to hear about your trip when you return," I declared. "I'll pray with you that God will make this a profitable trip, and that you'll have many witnessing opportunities."

"Someone said, 'There are risks when you follow the

Lord.' But I don't believe that." Peter added, "There is no safer place to be than walking in obedience with the Lord. When you're in step with God, it's a matter of faith."

Looking Back

As I look back I ask myself, *Is this the same young man that visited our church and hated it?* It shows what happens when the Spirit of God is allowed to take over in a person's life.

Recently someone asked Peter, "Are you doing full-time Christian work?"

I loved his answer. He replied, "Is there any other kind?"

To think this young man has only been a Christian for four years is amazing. The maturity he has is truly a miracle of God. It's refreshing to see a young man only twenty-one years of age so enthusiastic about following the Lord and doing his will.

As I was reviewing this story with Dawn, she related to me that the only reason she visited our church was to get me off her back.

I laughed and said, "I thought I was being an encourager."

"I know now, however, that God was in it. The results are the proof," she declared.

As Dawn was reflecting back on God's workings in her life, she recalled the many times he had nudged her to follow him. "I kept putting him off. I remember once when I was late for a tennis match, I grabbed a sweater and started to run. I tripped and fell from the top of the stairs to the bottom. I knew I was hurt and I sensed God's presence. I remember saying, 'Not now God, I'm too busy.'

"I was able to get up and call an ambulance. I will never forget the trip to the hospital. A woman came along with the paramedics and all she said to me was, 'Young lady, you need to trust the Lord.'

"As I was carried out of the ambulance, I turned to the woman and asked, 'May I see you again?'"

"'No, you'll probably never see me again. Just remember what I said.'"

"I have often wondered," Dawn mused, "if God sent that woman to warn me. You see, Nellie, even though I was desperate that day at Bible study, I really wasn't ready to receive Christ until then. I know there were other times when I ignored God's promptings. I'm glad he didn't give up on me."

"God's mercy and grace is something we cannot understand. We know we don't deserve it," I said. "We just accept it with gratefulness of heart. It is something I never want to take for granted."

"Let me tell you what happened recently," Dawn went on. "I was thinking about the goodness of the Lord, and all he had done for me. Then I pictured myself leaving the church. I was wearing a new white robe. My old clothes were all in a heap on the ground. I was new. All the hollow emptiness within me was gone. It was all behind me.

"As I sat in church the following Sunday, I said to the Lord, 'I must really love you to be sitting in such an ugly church.'"

I was flabbergasted, "Dawn," I protested, "I think we have a beautiful church."

"Being a decorator, I've always dreamed of worshiping in a cathedral-type church," she said. "I love the magnificent church structure, the majestic beauty, and the stained-glass windows. I also love the stone carvings on the buildings."

"But don't worship a *building*," I explained. "The building isn't the church. Do you know that many of the cathedrals of old symbolized the power of the church and the pride and wealth of the town in which it was built? That isn't what Christianity is all about."

"Oh, yes, I see that now," Dawn said. "The beauty is not

155

in the building but in the people who worship there. They are the true church since they are the body of Christ.

"I must admit," she went on, "I loved all the trappings, the pomp and the ceremony. But now I've shed my dirty clothes and put on a white robe. I'm free! I'm clean! and I'm living for the Lord."

One of the most effective ways of reaching people for Christ is through informal neighborhood Bible studies—all who can, should get involved.

Christians can bring their neighbors who may be churchgoers but haven't the slightest idea how to be in the family of God. Many people feel that because they are regular church attenders they automatically are a candidate for heaven. The disappointment comes when the emptiness of ritualistic services does not meet the needs of their hearts. We must point them to the Savior.

A woman in our Bible class confided in me one day, "I have gone to church all of my life and I don't know anything about the Bible. How is it that you know so much? Have you gone to school to learn these things?

"No," I answered. "I've read the Scriptures since I was a little girl. We have had excellent Bible teaching both at our church and in my home. My Sunday school teachers encouraged every one in the class to memorize verses from the Bible. It's been a continual learning process. It's the best education I've ever had."

We as believers in an evangelical church must be careful we don't get inbred. It is so easy to attend every meeting in our own church. Having fellowship with God's people is wonderful, but we must not forget our neighbors and those we rub elbows with from day to day.

21

What Would You Have Said—

When Someone Said, "Jesus Is Out on the Stoop. I Haven't Invited Him In Yet"?

Lynn

I wasn't sure about Lynn. She faithfully attended our Bible class but never participated in our discussion and never asked questions. It isn't as though she were unfriendly or shy, but it was as though she didn't want to get involved. Many of the women weren't knowledgeable about the Bible but at least they would ask questions—not Lynn. By the expression on her face I knew she was interested, but she didn't say a word. I knew better than to ask her any question during class.

One time we were discussing Revelation 3:20. Jesus was

saying, "'Here I am! I stand at the door and knock. If any-one hears my voice and opens the door, I will come in and eat with him, and he with me.'"

"Jesus wants us to have fellowship with him," I explained. "And he wants us to include him in the things we do.

"Going to church and Bible studies is a great way to learn, but it's what we *do* with what we learn that counts. In other words we have to apply the Scripture to our lives.

"When our two oldest children Karen and Tim were twelve and ten years old, respectively, they entered a con-test in Junior Church. The purpose was to encourage the memorization of Scripture. The persons who learned the verses in the category of their choice got a prize. Each cate-gory had a number of verses to be memorized. To be a pri-vate, ten verses had to be learned. To be a corporal, more were added until it came to the general. To attain that rank a person had to learn three hundred and fifty verses. Now that's quite a feat for these young people.

"'Which category are you going to shoot for?' I asked Karen.

"'I'm going to be a general,' she said.

"'What about you, Tim?' I asked.

"'General, of course.' He wasn't going to let his older sister get ahead of him.

"Three hundred and fifty verses is a lot to learn," I told the class." You might even be tempted to think, *They'll get a lot of credit for heaven if they do that*. But as much as God wants us to memorize his Word, it's the obeying and applying his Word that pleases him. You see, God looks at the heart. There had to be a purpose other than winning in a contest. As time went on my children learned that, too. Oh, yes, we helped them and drilled them. We prayed that they would take to heart what they had learned and apply it to their everyday life.

"Jesus is saying he wants to be a part of our life. He won't force his way; he's waiting for an invitation."

Lynn hung around after class was over. It seemed as though she wanted to talk but was hesitant.

"Lynn," I said, "you've been attending class for some time now, but we haven't talked much. Tell me, have you ever invited Jesus Christ into your life?"

"He's out on the stoop," she said nervously. "You know what I mean—he's still out on the porch. I haven't invited him in yet."

"Is that what you do to your friends who knock on your door? Keep them standing out on the porch?" I asked.

"Of course not!" She seemed insulted. "I . . . that is, I invite them in. I see what you mean," she said. "I've got to go now. I'll see you next week." And off she went.

I prayed for Lynn that week. She seemed so close and yet. . . .

We were about ready to start class the following week when Lynn rushed in. She came right over to me and said in an excited voice, "Jesus is no longer out on the stoop, he's in my house. I invited him into my life this week, and I want him to be a part of everything I do from now on. I feel like a different person. Many things have been settled for me this week.

"I didn't tell you but we'll be moving to another state soon. I was very unhappy about it, but now that Jesus Christ is in my life it's going to be okay. I will now be better able to face the future. Thanks for the challenge of last week."

Looking Back

When God's Word is released, the Holy Spirit can activate the seed that's been sown in the heart. He has something to work with. It's not our opinions that matter but

God's Word. It's powerful. But a person cannot come to Christ apart from hearing the Word of God. That's how we get faith (*see* Rom. 10:17).

If we are to be effective in our witness for Christ, we need to hide God's Word in our own hearts, obey it, and apply it. Then we will be equipped to share the gospel.

22

What Would You Have Said—

When a Christian School Student Told You She Was a Hypocrite?

Mindy

I saw the young teenage girl head for the front of the auditorium. The speaker at the Bible conference had invited those who wanted to receive Christ as Savior to come forward.

"Counseling will be available at the close of the service," he explained.

She did not walk over to him but stood off at the side by herself. She was sobbing and seemed devastated.

The speaker nodded for me to go and speak to her. I approached her gently.

"Would you like to talk?" I asked.

"I need desperately to talk to someone. I am absolutely miserable."

"What prompted you to come forward?" I asked.

"I'm confused," she said. "I don't think I've ever really accepted Christ as my Savior. I think I've just been playing around at being a Christian. You see I've always attended a Christian school. I know all the right words, but I know my heart isn't right before God."

"Is that why you came forward—to make things right with God?" I asked.

"I can't stand living another day with the guilt of being a fraud. I've just been playacting. I realize for the first time that I, Mindy, am a hypocrite and I hate it. Please help me to make things right with God. I want to live a good Christian life."

"If you mean what you say you'll have no problem. The Bible tells us in Luke 19:10 that Jesus came to seek and to save the lost."

"That's me," she wept. "I'm lost."

"Mindy, do you know why Jesus Christ died on the cross?"

"Yes. He died on the cross for my sins. You see I know all that but until now I really wasn't interested. I wanted to have fun with my friends, but I'm not having fun because my insides aren't right."

"Do you know how to pray?" I asked.

"Yes," she seemed a little embarrassed. "I don't deserve God's forgiveness."

"None of us do," I replied. "It's only by his grace that we are saved. Grace means unmerited favor. We don't deserve salvation but because of his love he is willing to forgive us and even make us a member of his family—his royal family.

"First John 1:9 says: If we confess our sins, he is faithful and just and will forgive our sins and purify us from all unrighteousness.' Then in John 1:12 it says: 'Yet to all who received him, to those who believed in his name, he gave the right to become the children of God.'

"Are you ready to take that step of faith?" I asked.

"I really want to," she replied.

Mindy prayed and confessed her lack of dependence and trust in Jesus Christ. "I do trust you now and want to be in your family. Right now I receive Christ as my Savior. Please help me to live for you and be a good influence in the lives of my friends. Help me to tell them what I did today. In Jesus' name I pray, *Amen.*"

The lights in the auditorium dimmed. They were preparing to show a missionary film. Mindy and I left after deciding we would meet the following day.

I saw Mindy after breakfast.

"I looked for you after the film last night," she said. "I wanted so much to talk to you further. Can we go some place now?"

We found a corner in the lodge and sat down to chat.

"I'm so glad I made a decision to follow Christ last night. I feel so different. I feel so free, like a load has been lifted. It's like I'm a new person."

"You are a new person, a new person in Jesus Christ," I said. "This is just the beginning though. You took a step of faith last night. The Christian life is one step after another. To grow in Christ you need to begin reading your Bible on a daily basis. God's Word is nourishing. It's like food for your soul. It will make you a healthy Christian if you obey what it says."

"Do you have any Christian friends?" I asked. "I mean the kind that take their faith in Christ seriously."

"Yes, but most of them have been faking it like me. You see I always wanted to be popular. I know how to get attention. If I'm loud and act like a smart aleck people seem to like me and want to be around me. The problem is I don't like myself. I don't want to be that kind of a person.

"No one knows the hurt I have on the inside. I've kept it all to myself. My friends would be surprised if they knew how I really felt.

"My mother and father are divorced. My father abused her. I saw him hurt her. I'm glad she doesn't have to live with him any longer."

"Did your father ever abuse you?" I asked.

"Yes, and he still does," she said. "You see, I have to go and visit him regularly. I would run away if it wasn't for my younger sister and brother. If I don't go he will hurt them. I have to stand in their way."

"What do you mean by that?" I asked.

"My father has a violent temper. He hits and slaps us at the least little thing. Once when we were visiting him, he got mad at my little brother. He doubled up his fist and started toward him. I put my hand up to stop him, and he took my three fingers, bent them backward and broke them. It was absolutely awful. I hated him for that. Once he almost choked me to death."

"Does your mother know about this?" I asked.

"Yes, and she went to the judge to see if he could be denied visiting rights."

"Did the judge do anything for you?"

"No, he said my father still had the right to see his children. My mother cries when we visit him. She hasn't given up though; she's trying to get us help.

"Right now my biggest problem is the hatred and resentment I feel for my father. What can I do about it?"

"There are no easy answers," I replied. "I do know that hate and resentment eat away like a cancer and destroy our insides and are not the answer God would give. The Bible says in Luke 6:28 to do good to those who mistreat you. That's a hard saying. A thought just came to me. Jesus took our hate and replaced it with his love. Do you think you could replace your hate for your dad with pity? The turmoil you are experiencing will disappear. If your father sees your changed attitude, it might soften him. The time may come when you can tell him what Jesus Christ has done for you. In the meantime pray for your dad. He must be a very unhappy man."

164

"Do you think my father will ever change?" she asked.

"I don't know. It says in Matthew 19:26 '. . . with God all things are possible.' Take one step at a time. I will be praying with you. Even if it doesn't change him it will change you. You'll be a better person because you have forgiven your dad."

"What if Mom can get a restraining order, should I still see him?" she asked.

"My advice would be to accept the order if it comes through. That would be for your own safety and that of your brother and sister. If you are obliged to spend time with him, pray for God's guidance, wisdom, behavior, and protection."

"I'm so glad I came this weekend. My grandparents invited me. In fact my whole family was here last Friday. I was the only one who chose to stay. I'm glad I did. I feel for the first time I have some direction in life."

"You'll be returning to school next week. You are attending one of the finest Christian schools in the country. Why don't you have a talk with your counselor? I'm sure you'll find her to be a good friend."

"Yes, I think I'll be comfortable with that. My new goal in life is to live for Christ."

Looking Back

Attending a Christian school gives the student an opportunity to be exposed to spiritual matters. But it is no guarantee that he or she will embrace the teaching it affords. The good part is students are constantly being reminded what the Word of God says. The Spirit of God then has something to activate. Mindy was miserable because having been taught in the Word, she knew what the Christian behavior should be. On the outside she felt she measured up, but her heart betrayed her. "I feel awful," she said.

I recently visited my daughter Karen in Boston. It was

her birthday. I told her she needn't make any rich desserts for us since I had just recently discovered my cholesterol level was a bit elevated. We began to discuss the no-cholesterol foods on the market. My seven-year-old granddaughter, Elizabeth, was listening intently.

"Mom, may I go to the store with Grandpa?" she asked, "It's your birthday you know."

Karen smiled and said, "Don't be gone too long."

When she returned, her friend Lindsay was waiting for her.

"I feel so good on the inside," Elizabeth excitedly said to her friend. I just bought my mother a birthday present with my own money. It was something she needed badly. I want my grandmother to see it before I wrap it."

I went upstairs with her and she took the present out of the bag. It was a package of no-cholesterol muffins. She was so proud. I didn't have the heart to tell her I was the one, not her mother, that had the cholesterol problem. She felt so good on the inside because she wanted to please her mother and she knew that was right.

Admitting to being a hypocrite wasn't easy for Mindy. But living with that burden was eating away at her insides. Only the cleansing blood of Jesus Christ could wipe away the guilt and misery of her young life. When she confessed her sin and received Jesus Christ as her Savior she was transformed; she was a new person. She felt good on the inside. Her new goal was to please the Lord.

23

What Would You Have Said—

When Someone Suggested That You Sell Baseball Cards at Your Church?

"I'd like to surprise Nathaniel and get him some baseball cards for his birthday," my husband said. "Look at this ad. Seems like there's going to be a big sale. Why don't you go with me?"

"But it's way over on the east side of Detroit. It must be thirty miles away," I said without enthusiasm.

"Oh, come on. Isn't your grandson worth it? It will be an opportunity to show him love. You should have seen how excited he was when he showed me his collection. Come on, get your coat. I'll take you out to lunch afterward."

All of a sudden it wasn't so far after all!

I was surprised to see the big crowd gathered in the hotel room where they were selling the cards. We had no idea there would be so many interested people.

I wasn't interested in looking at the cards (and besides the room was already crowded) so I stayed out in the lobby. I noticed several grown men sitting on the sofa trading cards. It struck me as rather peculiar.

One of the men noticed me so I smiled and said, "I thought this was for kids. I didn't think grown-ups would be interested in trading baseball cards."

"Oh," he explained, "this is big business. I've been doing this for years. I've made lots of money." He explained that the value of the cards depended on the status of the player.

"How about Frank Tanana?" I asked. "Where does he stand?"

"He's not a superstar yet but he's valuable."

"Well, in my book he's a superstar. He's one of the finest people I know. He belongs to our church," I said.

"Then you've got it made," he declared. "You go in there and buy all the Tanana cards you can get and sell them to the people in your church for twice what you paid. You'll make yourself some money. I guarantee it. You'll make money."

"No, I'd never do that. That's not what church is all about," I protested.

"I go to church, and I'd do that," he insisted. "Let me tell you," he went on, "I went through the whole bit. I was baptized and confirmed and I even memorized some verses in the psalms. I still go to church every Sunday."

"Do you read the Bible?" I asked.

"Oh, no, I did that when I was a kid. I don't need to do that now. What about you," he asked, "what's your thing?"

"My *thing*? Well, I love to tell people how they can have a relationship with Jesus Christ," I said. "You see there's more to Christianity than being confirmed and baptized. God wants to have fellowship with you on a daily basis."

"I pray every day," he said.

"But you just told me you don't read your Bible. You know God wants to speak to you, too, and he does through the Bible. That's how he gives direction and guidance for life. It's really his love letter to believers," I explained.

"You mean I should be reading my Bible every day?" he seemed puzzled.

"Absolutely. To be a *Christian* is not just a course in catechism. It's an on-going relationship. How about getting back to reading your Bible tomorrow morning? Start in the Book of John."

"I won't need to read it tomorrow, because it's Sunday and I go to church. But I could start on Monday."

"I guarantee it will change your life," I said. "It has revolutionized mine and the lives of many other people I know."

"Yeah, I can see you're excited about it."

"It's a lot more exciting than baseball cards."

My husband then arrived on the scene. I introduced them and told Paul what we had been talking about. He then added his testimony to what I had said.

Looking Back

It was just a nudge to a stranger. The man was much younger than I, and my husband was nearby so I felt comfortable talking with him. We need to take every opportunity to talk about the Lord and to encourage people to read the Word of God so they can discover God's truth for themselves.

24

What Would You Have Said—

When the Scientist Said, "I'm an Atheist. I Believe Only in Scientific Facts"?

While at poolside one of my neighbors, a professional near retirement age, said to me recently, "I haven't seen you at the tennis courts this year. I saw you a lot last season but I don't think I've seen you at all this year. Aren't you playing anymore?"

"I still play but I've been rather busy lately."

"What have you been doing with yourself?" he asked.

"I've been busy speaking and doing some writing," I replied.

He seemed curious and asked, "What kind of speaking do you do?"

"I speak about God's dealings in people's lives. My speaking is all Bible based; that is, the Bible is my authority. It's very exciting."

170

"I don't believe in the Bible," he said. "I don't even believe in God. I believe in scientific facts. God just doesn't fit in to my way of thinking."

"I would think the very fact that you are a scientist would be proof enough. Why, doing research every day would leave no doubt that God exists," I said.

"Well, if there is a God, why doesn't he do something about the starving people around the world? People like the animists who don't know about God?" He sounded annoyed.

"Now wait a minute. There isn't anyone that has an excuse. The Bible says in Romans, chapter one, that what has been known about God has been made plain. For since the creation of the world God's invisible qualities—his eternal power and his divine nature—have been clearly seen, being understood by what has been made. Therefore men are without excuse. Actually man suppressed the truth about God. They didn't want to believe. They chose to rebel against God."

"What if they didn't know any better?"

"God will hold them responsible for the light they have been given. As I said, creation is evidence there is a God."

"Well, I think God should take care of the starving people in the world," he continued.

"Here you are, a mere man telling God how he should run his universe. It reminds me of the verse (Isaiah 45:9): 'Does the clay say to the potter, 'What are you making?''

He didn't get the point, but continued making accusations about God. He was not angry. I believe he was trying in a friendly way to trap me. After all he was a scientist, and who was I?

What he didn't know was the power of God. I didn't feel a bit intimidated.

"The animists don't know about God," he said, "so I don't think it's fair. And another thing, why have the Jews suffered so much? I just don't understand it."

"I believe God is trying to get their attention. He wants the Jews to turn to him in repentance. The Bible says so in Second Chronicles 7:14: 'If my people who are called by name, will humble themselves and pray and seek my face and turn from their wicked ways, then will I hear from heaven and will forgive their sin and will heal their land.'

"By the way," I said, "are you Jewish?"

"Yes, I am."

"You have been talking about people who haven't had a chance to hear about God. *You* don't have that excuse, do you? I believe you just refuse to believe.

"God says you have a choice." I said. "He says in Joshua 24:15: '. . . choose for yourselves this day whom you will serve. . . .' You see the problem is that man has chosen to go his own way. The Bible says in Romans 1:20, 21 that man is without excuse.

"You have been talking about the people who haven't had a chance to hear about God," I said. "The Jews have had many chances. Just think of the privilege God afforded them by giving them his Oracles. They were indeed a blessed people, and yet so many refuse to believe and don't give thanks to their Creator. That's hard for me to comprehend.

"One of my greatest disappointments in talking to Jewish people is they don't know their Scriptures, the Old Testament. I would love to discuss it with them but they are ignorant of it. They are knowledgeable about so many things, even outstanding. I would go as far as to say they are brilliant except for the most important thing in life—God. The Jews have a marvelous heritage. I would think they'd want to know more about it."

"I just don't believe there is a God who created the universe. It's just not possible," he declared.

"The watch you're wearing," I said, "that just came into existence by itself? There isn't such a thing as a watchmaker, right? I suppose it stands to reason because my mind can't conceive of making a watch, it just couldn't happen. But you're wearing it, and it works."

My neighbor had no answers. He stood up to leave. Then he surprised me by saying, "My wife and I will be going to Russia, Poland, and other parts of Europe. We'll be back in about six weeks. When I get back I would like to talk to you further. I am very interested in what you have been saying. Maybe I'm really not an atheist—maybe I'm an agnostic."

"There might be hope for you yet," I teased. "An atheist refuses to believe in God. An agnostic just doesn't know. A smart man like you should look into it."

We had a stimulating discussion without being angry. He was an intelligent man, but his reasoning about God was faulty. I am praying that God will give him a hunger to know his Word, and that he will want to know God.

Looking Back

As I've finished the last chapter of this book. I would like to turn the question back to my reader. What would you have said in these situations? We may not have the answers beforehand. The Spirit of God leads us. Remember the words of Jesus: "But the Counselor, the Holy Spirit, whom the Father will send in my name, will teach you all things and will remind you of everything I have said to you" (John 14:26).

We can only remember what we have read and studied. The Bible says to ". . . always be prepared to give an answer to everyone who asks you to give the reason for the hope that you have. But do this with gentleness and respect" (1 Peter 3:15).

Think about it. Be prepared and take a step of faith.

There is a price to pay when you're available to God for witnessing, however. You might get so excited about sharing the gospel while doing your grocery shopping that you forget to take your groceries home! That happened to me the other day. Of course it was the first time it ever happened but that's the cost of enjoying God's work to the fullest.